Capitalism: A Very Short Introduction

VERY SHORT INTRODUCTIONS are for anyone wanting a stimulating and accessible way in to a new subject. They are written by experts, and have been published in more than 25 languages worldwide.

The series began in 1995, and now represents a wide variety of topics in history, philosophy, religion, science, and the humanities. Over the next few years it will grow to a library of around 200 volumes – a Very Short Introduction to everything from ancient Egypt and Indian philosophy to conceptual art and cosmology.

Very Short Introductions available now:

Available soon:

For more information visit our web site

www.oup.co.uk/vsi

James Fulcher

CAPITALISM

A Very Short Introduction

OXFORD
UNIVERSITY PRESS

OXFORD
UNIVERSITY PRESS

Great Clarendon Street, Oxford OX2 6DP

Oxford University Press is a department of the University of Oxford.
It furthers the University's objective of excellence in research, scholarship,
and education by publishing worldwide in

Oxford New York

Auckland Bangkok Buenos Aires Cape Town Chennai
Dar es Salaam Delhi Hong Kong Istanbul Karachi Kolkata
Kuala Lumpur Madrid Melbourne Mexico City Mumbai Nairobi
São Paulo Shanghai Taipei Tokyo Toronto

Oxford is a registered trade mark of Oxford University Press
in the UK and in certain other countries

Published in the United States
by Oxford University Press Inc., New York

© James Fulcher 2004

British Library Cataloguing in Publication Data

Data available

Library of Congress Cataloging in Publication Data

Data available

ISBN 0-19-280218-6

1 3 5 7 9 10 8 6 4 2

Typeset by RefineCatch Ltd, Bungay, Suffolk
Printed in Great Britain by
TJ International Ltd., Padstow, Cornwall

Acknowledgment

I would like to acknowledge the support given to me by the University of Leicester in granting me the study leave that enabled me to write this book.

Contents

List of illustrations

Chapter 1
What is capitalism?

Merchant capitalism

In April 1601 the English East India Company sent its first expedition to the East Indies. After some 18 months its four ships, *Ascension*, *Dragon*, *Hector*, and *Susan*, had returned from Sumatra and Java with a cargo mainly of pepper. The success of this venture led to a second expedition by the same ships, which left London in March 1604. On the return journey *Hector* and *Susan* set off first, but *Susan* was lost at sea and *Hector* was rescued by *Ascension* and *Dragon*, which found her drifting off South Africa with most of her crew dead. *Ascension*, *Dragon*, and *Hector* made it back to England in May 1606 with a cargo of pepper, cloves, and nutmegs. The shareholders in these two voyages made a profit of 95% on their investment.

Despite the similar success of the third expedition in 1607, the fourth one in 1608, consisting of the ships *Ascension* and *Union*, was a complete disaster. The *Ascension* reached the west coast of India but was there wrecked by its 'proud and headstrong master', who drove his ship aground after ignoring local warnings about shoaling waters. The *Union* called in at a Madagascan port, where the crew was ambushed and the captain killed, but nonetheless the ship made it to Sumatra and loaded a cargo. On her way back, the *Union* was wrecked off the coast of Brittany. The investors in this expedition lost all their capital.

Capitalism is essentially the investment of money in the expectation of making a profit, and huge profits could be made at some considerable risk by long-distance trading ventures of this kind. Profit was quite simply the result of scarcity and distance. It was made from the huge difference between the price paid for, say, pepper in the spice islands and the price it fetched in Europe, a difference that dwarfed the costs of the venture. What mattered was whether the cargo made it back to Europe, though market conditions were also very important, for the sudden return of a large fleet could depress prices. Markets could also become saturated if the high profitability of the trade led too many to enter it. A glut of pepper eventually forced the East India Company to diversify into other spices and other products, such as indigo.

A large amount of capital was needed for this trade. An *East Indianman*, as the ships engaged in this trade were called, had to be built, fitted out, armed with cannon against Dutch and Portuguese rivals, and repaired, if and when it returned. The Company's shipyards at Blackwall and Deptford, which were major employers of local labour, required financing. Capital was also needed to stock outgoing vessels with bullion and goods to pay for the spices, with munitions, and with food and drink for the large crews they carried. On the Company's third expedition, *Dragon* had a crew of 150, *Hector* 100, and *Consent* 30 – in all 280 mouths to feed, at least initially. One reason for the large crews was to make sure there were enough sailors to get the ships back after the hazards of the expedition had taken their toll.

The East India Company's capital was obtained largely but not entirely from the rich London merchants who controlled and administered it. Aristocrats and their hangers-on were another source, and one welcomed by the Company because of their influence at Court. The Company's privileges depended on royal favour. Foreign money was also involved, mainly from Dutch

2

1. **East Indiaman, 1829**

merchants excluded by the rival Dutch East Indies Company. They were also a useful source of intelligence about that company's activities.

The first 12 voyages were each financed separately, with capital committed to one voyage only and the profits of the voyage distributed among its shareholders, according to traditional merchant practices. This was, however, a risky way of financing long-distance trade, for it exposed capital to a long period of uncertainty in far-away and unknown places. Risk could be spread by sending out several ships on each expedition, so that not all the eggs were in one basket, but whole expeditions could, nonetheless, be lost, as in 1608. The company shifted to a method of finance that spread risks over a number of voyages and then became a fully fledged joint-stock company, with, after 1657, continuous investment unrelated to specific voyages. In 1688 trading in its stocks began on the London Stock Exchange.

Risk was also reduced through monopolistic practices. Like its counterparts abroad, the English East India Company was closely intertwined with the state, which granted it a monopoly for the import of oriental goods and gave it the right to export bullion to pay for them. In exchange the state, always short of money, gained revenue from customs duties on the large and valuable imports made by the company. There was certainly competition but it was international competition, in the Indies between the English, the Dutch, and the Portuguese, and as far as possible eliminated within each country. Outsiders were always trying to break into the trade, and one of the key privileges bestowed on the East India Company by the state was the right to take action against 'interlopers'.

Markets were manipulated by buying up stocks and holding back sales. In the 17th century Amsterdam merchants were particularly skilled in these practices and busily established monopolies not only in spices but in Swedish copper, whale products, Italian silks, sugar, perfume ingredients, and saltpetre (an ingredient of gunpowder). Large warehouses were crucial to this and Fernand Braudel comments that the warehouses of the Dutch merchants were bigger and more expensive than large ships. They could hold sufficient grain to feed the entire country for 10 to 12 years. This was not just a matter of holding goods back to force up prices, for large stocks also enabled the Dutch to destroy foreign competitors by suddenly flooding the whole European market with goods.

This was certainly capitalism, for long-distance trade required a heavy investment of capital in the expectation of large profits, but a free market capitalism it clearly was not. The secret of making high profits was to secure monopolies by one means or another, exclude competitors, and control markets in every way possible. Since profit was made from trading in scarce products rather than rationalizing production, the impact of merchant capitalism on society was limited. Most of the European population could get on with their daily work without being affected by the activities of these owners of capital.

Capitalist production

In the 1780s two Scots, James M'Connel and John Kennedy, travelled south to become apprentices in the Lancashire cotton industry. After gaining experience and making some money in the manufacture of cotton machinery, they set up their own firm in 1795 with an initial capital of £1,770. They soon made good profits from cotton spinning, achieving a return on capital of over 30% in 1799 and 1800. They accumulated capital rapidly and by 1800 their capital had risen to £22,000, by 1810 to £88,000. By 1820 the company had three mills and had established itself as the leading spinner of fine cotton in Manchester, the global metropolis of cotton spinning.

This soon became a very competitive industry, however, and profits could not be sustained at the high level of the early 1800s. This was, indeed, largely because high profits had resulted in expansion and attracted new entrants. There were already 344 cotton mills by 1819 but by 1839 there were 1,815. Technical advances enabled huge increases in productivity during the 1830s, and competition drove companies to invest heavily in the new machinery. The bigger mills built at this time contained 40,000 spindles, as compared with the 4,500 or so of their predecessors. The costs of this heavy investment in buildings and machinery, together with the downward pressure of increased productive capacity on yarn prices, depressed the industry's profitability to low levels in the 1830s.

Profit depended ultimately on the workers who turned raw cotton into yarn. M'Connel and Kennedy's labour force grew from 312 in 1802 to around 1,500 by the 1830s. Much of this was cheap child labour and at times nearly half those employed were under the age of 16. In 1819 there were 100 children under the age of 10, some as young as 7, who worked from 6.00 in the morning until 7.30 at night.

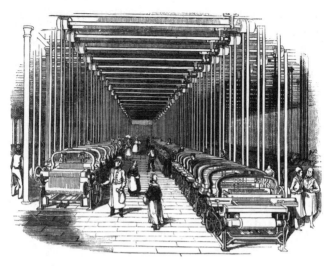

2. Power looms dominate a 19th-century cotton mill

Apart from the occasional heavy cost of new factories and new machinery, wages were the company's main cost. Its annual wage bill was over £35,000 by 1811 and over £48,000 by the mid-1830s. Wage costs were minimized not just by holding wage rates down but also by replacing craft workers with less skilled and cheaper labour, as the invention of automatic machinery made this possible. The cyclical instability of the industry resulted in periodic slumps in demand, which forced employers to reduce wages and hours in order to survive.

As industrial capitalism developed, conflict over wages became increasingly organized. The spinners defended themselves against wage reductions through their unions, organizing at first locally but then regionally and nationally. In 1810, 1818, and 1830 there were increasingly organized strikes, but these were defeated by the employers, with the assistance of the state, which arrested strikers and imprisoned union leaders. The employers had created their own associations, so that they could 'black-list' union militants, answer strikes with 'lock-outs', and provide mutual financial support. Vigorous action by the spinners' unions does seem, nonetheless, to have been quite successful, for wages remained stable, in spite of declining profitability and employers' attempts to reduce them.

The exploitation of labour was not just a matter of keeping the wage bill down but also involved the disciplining of the worker. Industrial capitalism required regular and continuous work, if costs were to be minimized. Expensive machinery had to be kept constantly in use. Idleness and drunkenness, even wandering around and conversation, could not be allowed. The cotton mills did indeed have trouble recruiting labour because people simply did not like long, uninterrupted shifts and close supervision. Employers had to find ways of enforcing a discipline that was quite alien to the first generation of industrial workers. They commonly used the crude and negative sanctions of corporal punishment (for children), fines, or the threat of dismissal, but some developed more sophisticated and moralistic ways of controlling their workers.

Robert Owen introduced 'silent monitors' at his New Lanark mills. Each worker had a piece of wood, with its sides painted black for bad work, blue for indifferent, yellow for good, and white for excellent. The side turned to the front provided a constant reminder, visible to all, of the quality of the previous day's work. Each department had a 'book of character' recording the daily colour for each worker. Discipline was not only a factory matter, for Owen also controlled the community. He sent round street patrols to report drunkenness and fined the drunks next morning. He insisted on cleanliness and established detailed rules for the cleaning of streets and houses. There was even a curfew that required everyone to be indoors after 10.30 p.m. in the winter.

As E. P. Thompson has emphasized, disciplined work was regular, timed work. It meant turning up every day, starting on time, and taking breaks of a specified length at specified times. Employers had a long battle against the well-established tradition of taking off, as additional 'saint's days', 'St Monday', and even 'St Tuesday', to recover from weekend drinking. Time became a battleground, with some unscrupulous employers putting clocks forward in the morning and back at night. There are stories of watches being taken off workers, so that the employer's control of time could not be challenged. Significantly, timepiece ownership spread at the same time as the Industrial Revolution and at the end of the 18th century the government tried to tax the ownership of clocks and watches.

Industrial capitalism not only created work, it also created 'leisure' in the modern sense of the term. This might seem surprising, for the early cotton masters wanted to keep their machinery running as long as possible and forced their employees to work very long hours. However, by requiring continuous work during work hours and ruling out non-work activity, employers had separated out leisure from work. Some did this quite explicitly by creating distinct holiday periods, when factories were shut down, because it was better to do this than have work disrupted by the casual taking of days off. 'Leisure' as a distinct non-work time, whether in the form of the holiday, weekend, or evening, was a result of the disciplined and bounded work time created by capitalist production. Workers then wanted more leisure and leisure time was enlarged by union campaigns, which first started in the cotton industry, and eventually new laws were passed that limited the hours of work and gave workers holiday entitlements.

Leisure was also the creation of capitalism in another sense, through the commercialization of leisure. This no longer meant participation in traditional sports and pastimes. Workers began to pay for leisure activities organized by capitalist enterprises. The new railway companies provided cheap excursion tickets and Lancashire cotton workers could go to Blackpool for the day. In 1841 Thomas Cook organized his first tour, an excursion by rail from Leicester to Loughborough for a temperance meeting. Mass travel to spectator sports, especially football and horse-racing, where people could be charged for entry, was now possible. The importance of this can hardly be exaggerated, for whole new industries were emerging to exploit and develop the leisure market, which was to become a huge source of consumer demand, employment, and profit.

Capitalist production had transformed people's work and leisure lives. The investment of capital in the expectation of profit drove the Industrial Revolution and rapid technical progress increased productivity by leaps and bounds. But machines could not work on their own and it was wage labour that was central to the making of profit. The wage bill was the employer's main cost and became the focus of the conflict between the owners of capital and, as Karl Marx put it, those who owned only their 'labour power', the capacity to make money through physical work. Workers were concentrated in factories and mills, where they had to work in a continuous and disciplined manner under the supervisor's watchful eye, but also now had an opportunity to organize themselves collectively in unions. Non-work activities were expelled from work time into leisure time and daily life was now sharply divided between work and leisure. Wage labour also meant, however, that workers had money to spend on their leisure life. The commercialization of leisure created new industries that fed back into the expansion of capitalist production.

Financial capitalism

On Thursday, 23 February 1995, Nick Leeson, the manager of Baring Securities in Singapore, watched the Nikkei, the Japanese stock market index, drop 330 points. In that one day, Barings lost £143 million through the deals that he had made, though he was the only one who knew what was happening. These losses came on top of the earlier ones of some £470 million that Leeson had kept hidden from his bosses. He knew the game was up and bolted, with his wife, to a hideaway on the north coast of Borneo. Meanwhile,

Barings managers, puzzling over the large sums of money that had gone missing in Singapore, tried desperately to find him. By the next morning it was clear that Baring Brothers, the oldest merchant bank in London, had sustained such huge losses that it was effectively bankrupt. Leeson tried to find his way back to England but was arrested in Frankfurt, extradited by Singapore for breaches of its financial regulations, and jailed for six and a half years.

Leeson had been trading in 'derivatives'. These are sophisticated financial instruments that *derive* their value from the value of something else, such as shares, bonds, currencies, or indeed commodities, such as oil or coffee. *Futures*, for example, are contracts to buy shares, bonds, currencies, or commodities at their *current* price at some point in the future. If you think that the price of a share is going to rise, you can buy a three months' future in it. After the three months have expired, you receive shares at the original price and make a profit by selling them at the higher price now prevailing. You can also buy *options*, which do not commit you to the future deal but allow you to decide later whether you want to go ahead or not.

The buying of futures can perform a very important function, since it enables the reduction of uncertainty and therefore risk. If the price of corn is high but the harvest is some way off, a farmer can lock into the existing price by making a deal with a merchant to sell the corn at this price in three months' time. Futures can also, however, be bought for purely speculative reasons to make money out of movements in prices. Financial futures of the kind that Leeson was trading in were more or less informed gambles on future price movements. This was what Susan Strange has called 'casino capitalism'.

Money could also be made from 'arbitrage', which exploits the small price differences that occur for technical reasons between markets. If you are able to spot these differences, calculate rapidly what they are worth, and move large sums of money very quickly, you can

(a) Above: Barings' 'star trader' Nick Leeson, after his release from prison in 1999

(b) Left: The 7th Baron Ashburton, Chairman of Barings at the time when Nick Leeson joined the company

3. The old and new faces of British financial capitalism

make big profits this way. Leeson found that he could exploit small differences, lasting less than a minute, between futures prices on the Osaka and Singapore stock exchanges. Operations of this kind could be carried out with little risk, since an immediate and calculable profit was taken from an existing, if short-lived, price difference.

Why then did things go so wrong for Leeson? He started down a slippery slope when he created a special error account, no. 88888, supposedly to handle innocent dealing and accountancy mistakes. This was the place where he hid his losses and he also found a way of concealing the accumulated end-of-the-month deficits by getting the Singapore 'back office' to make temporary but illegal transfers of money between various accounts. This and other manipulations bamboozled the auditors, who should have uncovered what was going on.

The existence of 88888 allowed Leeson to gamble with Barings' money. He could build his reputation by taking risks and trading aggressively on the futures markets, since any losses could be hidden. These *could* be covered by later trades and at one time he came close to breaking even, but if he had then closed 88888 down this would have ended the operation that made him the star dealer of Barings. Eventually his losses built up again and accumulated to the point at which they could no longer be concealed just by switching money around.

At this point he plunged into selling options, which, unlike futures, could immediately raise money to cover the monthly shortfalls in 88888. Leeson was gambling heavily on future price movements and the Tokyo stock market went the wrong way. As his losses increased, he raised the stakes by selling more and riskier options, supposedly on behalf of a mythical client called Philippe. When the Nikkei fell after the Kobe earthquake, his losses became so great that he tried single-handedly to force the market up by buying large numbers of futures. The downward pressures were far too strong and the market fell. By now, the losses and liabilities that he had built up were greater than the total capital of Barings.

Why did Barings allow all this to happen? They were a merchant bank which in 1984 had ventured into stockbroking by creating Baring Securities. This was a successful move and by 1989 dealings in mainly Japanese stocks and shares were accounting for half Barings' profits. Baring Securities then moved into the increasingly fashionable activity of derivatives trading. In 1993 Barings merged its capital with that of Barings Securities and in doing so fatally removed the 'fire-wall' protecting the bank from possible losses by its securities department. This was a particularly dangerous thing to do, since senior Barings managers had a poor grasp of the new game that they had entered, while no proper management structure had been put in place and financial controls were very weak. Fraud was an ever-present danger in this financially very complex world and Barings broke a golden rule by allowing Leeson to be both a trader and the manager of the Singapore 'back office', which checked the trades and balanced the books.

Leeson was apparently a very successful dealer who was making large profits for Barings and they backed him to the hilt. Ironically, when Barings crashed his bosses had just decided to reward his 1994 activities with a £450,000 bonus. As Leeson's operations drained increasing amounts of money from London and sent Barings hunting for loans around the world to cover them, Leeson's bosses actually thought they were financing profitable deals made by their star trader. It was not only the complexities of the financial markets and the extraordinarily weak financial controls within Barings that enabled Leeson to get away with things for so long, but also the corporate hunger for ever greater profits.

What then is capitalism?

We have examined three very different examples of capitalism. The various business activities involved are about as different as they could be, but all involve the investment of money in order to make a profit, the essential feature of capitalism. It is not the nature of the activity itself that matters but the possibility of making profit out of it. Indeed, it is typical of a capitalist society that virtually all economic activities that go on within it are driven by the opportunity to make profit out of capital invested in them.

Capital is money that is invested in order to make more money. By extension the term capital is often used to refer to money that is *available* for investment or, indeed, any asset that can be readily turned into money for it. Thus, a person's house is often described as their capital, because they can turn it into capital either by selling it or by borrowing on the strength of it. Many small businesses are indeed set up in this way. It is, however, only possible to turn property into capital if its ownership is clearly established, its value can be measured, its title can be transferred, and a market exists for it. A characteristic feature of the development of capitalist societies is the emergence of institutions that enable the conversion of assets of all kinds into capital. Hernando de Soto has argued persuasively that it is the absence of these institutions, above all functioning systems of property law, that frustrates the emergence of local capitalisms in the Third World. He claims that an enormous amount of value that is locked up in property cannot therefore be realized and put by entrepreneurs to productive use.

Capitalists existed before capitalism proper. Since the earliest times merchants have made money by investing in goods that they sold at a profit. As we saw with the East India Company, a merchant capitalism of this kind could be highly organized and very profitable, but it was an activity that involved only a small part of the economy. Most people's livelihoods did not come from economic activities financed by the investment of capital. In capitalism proper the whole economy becomes dependent on the investment of capital and this occurs when it is not just trade that is financed in this way but production as well.

Capitalist production is based on wage labour. A clear line of division and conflict emerges between the owners of capital, who own what Karl Marx called 'the means of production', and those who sell their labour in exchange for wages. The means of production are the workplace, the machinery, and the raw materials, which in pre-capitalist societies were owned not by the owners of capital but by the craftsmen who made the goods. A wage (or salary) is the price paid by the employer for labour sold by the worker. Just as a capitalist will invest money in any activity that brings a profit, a worker can find employment in any activity that pays a wage.

In a capitalist society, both capital and labour have an abstract and disembedded quality, since both are separated from specific economic activities and are therefore able in principle to move into any activity that suitably rewards them. In real life this mobility is constrained by the existing skills and experience of both the owners of capital and workers, and by the relationships and attachments that they have formed. The potential mobility of capital and labour is, nonetheless, one of the features of capitalist societies that gives them their characteristic dynamism.

Wage labour is both free and unfree. Unlike slaves, who are forced to work by their owners, wage labourers can decide whether they work and for whom. Unlike the serfs in feudal society, who were tied to their lord's land, they can move freely and seek work wherever they choose. These freedoms are, on the other hand, somewhat illusory, since in a capitalist society it is difficult to survive without paid work and little choice of work or employer may be available. Wage labourers are also subject to tight control by the employer and, as we saw in the cotton mills, capitalist production meant a new kind of disciplined and continuous work. Workers had become, as Marx put it, 'wage slaves'.

The importance of wage labour is not only its role in production but also its role in consumption. Wage labourers cannot themselves produce what they need or may wish to consume, they have to buy it, thereby providing the demand that activates a whole range of new capitalist enterprises. This applies not only to their food and clothing and personal possessions but to their leisure activities as well. As we saw earlier, capitalist production rapidly led to the creation of whole new industries based on the commercialization of leisure. This double role of wage labour, which enabled the dynamic interaction of production and consumption, explains why capitalist production expanded so very rapidly once it had got going.

Markets, like merchants, are nothing new, but they are central to a capitalist society in a quite new and more abstract way. This is because production and consumption are divorced – people do not consume what they produce or produce what they consume – and are linked only through the markets where goods and services are bought and sold. Instead of being a place where you can buy some extra item that you do not produce yourself, markets become the only means by which you can obtain anything. They are no longer located just in market-places but exist wherever buyers and sellers make their exchanges and, nowadays, this commonly means in some electronic space where prices are listed and deals registered. This applies not only to goods and services but also to labour, money, and capital. The wage, that is the price, for labour is established on a labour market, where employers compete for labour and workers compete for jobs. Money itself is bought and sold on currency markets. The ownership of companies is bought and sold in stock exchanges.

As we saw with the cotton mills, markets generate intense competition between capitalist enterprises. They compete in many different ways by, for example, exploiting labour more efficiently or using technical innovation to reduce costs or market products more effectively. Competition forces companies into constant change as they seek to beat the competition or at least keep up with it. Some of course fail and go under, throwing their employees out of work. This competitiveness, which contrasts strongly with the monopolistic practices of merchant capitalism, makes capitalist production exceptionally dynamic.

Capitalist enterprises have, nonetheless, found ways of reducing competition. Those with an edge over their rivals may relish the cut and thrust of competition, but this also creates uncertainty, reduces profits, and causes bankruptcies. Companies thus form trade associations to regulate competition. The market can be rigged by agreeing not to engage in price competition or deciding that all will pay the same wage rates. Competition can also be reduced by mergers and take-overs which concentrate production in fewer hands. There is in capitalism always a tension between competition and concentration, which are equally characteristic of it.

Since prices change, any market provides an opportunity to make money through speculation. This occurs when something is bought in the expectation of selling it, without increasing its value by processing it in some way, at a higher price in the future. It can occur in relation to almost any commodity. It may be grain, it may be a currency, it may be a derivative, it may be a slave. Speculation of this kind is often regarded as an unproductive and parasitic activity that is wholly separable from the real economy where goods and services are produced. Unproductive it may often be, but it is not just a means of making money through speculation but also a way of avoiding risk. Since the relationship between supply and demand is always changing, markets are unstable. The building up and storage of stocks is a means of insuring against some adverse price movement that could destroy profit and wipe out a business. Trading in futures, of the kind that Leeson speculated in, is another way of reducing uncertainty and originated long ago as a sophisticated way of protecting producers and traders against unpredictable future movements in prices.

The huge growth in the trading of currency during the 1980s and 1990s followed the shift from fixed to floating exchange rates in the 1970s, which created much greater uncertainty about future currency values. One way of reducing this uncertainty was to 'hedge' one's bets by buying currency futures. So, though the vast bulk of trading in currency futures is undoubtedly speculative, the expansion of this market and the financial innovations associated with it were grounded in real economic needs.

The same argument applies to the speculative trading of company shares. The existence of markets for capital is central to capitalism. They are essential to its functioning since they bring together those seeking to finance economic activities and those with money to invest. Since the stock market prices of companies change, as their economic situation and profitability changes, there are inevitably opportunities for speculating on future price movements. Speculation is not something separate from capitalism but an inevitable outgrowth of its essential machinery.

So, the answer to our question is that capitalism involves the investment of money to make more money. While merchants have long done this, it is when production is financed in this way that a transformative capitalism comes into being. Capitalist production depends on the exploitation of wage labour, which also fuels the consumption of the goods and services produced by capitalist enterprises. Production and consumption are linked by the markets that come to mediate all economic activities. Markets enable competition between enterprises but also generate tendencies towards concentration in order to reduce uncertainty. Market fluctuations also provide the basis of a speculative form of capitalism, which may not be productive but is, nonetheless, based on mechanisms that are central to the operation of a capitalist economy.

Chapter 2
Where did capitalism come from?

Capitalism made its breakthrough in Britain. So it is logical to ask what it was about Britain that provided particularly fertile ground for its growth. Indeed, some accounts of the origins of capitalism content themselves with answering this question. Ellen Meiksins Wood's recent book finds its origin in England and, perhaps surprisingly, in agriculture, in the relationships between landlords, tenants, and peasants. The first section of this chapter pursues a similar line of argument that owes much to her approach. But can we stop there? This chapter goes on to argue that capitalism must be seen ultimately as a European phenomenon. In exploring the origins of capitalism, the question is not so much why it developed in Britain but why it emerged in Europe.

Why Britain?

Britain in the 19th century was the first industrial society, but it was the breakthrough of capitalism in the 18th century that made 19th-century industrialism possible. The spread of market relationships and the growth of consumption generated a large enough demand to make investment in industrial production worthwhile. The need to earn money to spend on goods made people seek industrial employment, even though industrial work was monotonous and factory conditions were often grim. The control of labour by the owners of capital enabled them to increase productivity by concentrating workers in factories, introducing machinery and organizing labour in new ways.

Relationships between employers and workers in the 18th century already provide clear evidence of capitalist relationships. Trade unions and industrial conflict are generally associated with the 19th century, but organized conflicts of interest between labour and capital were already occurring in the 18th. During this century most craft workers organized themselves at some stage into 'combinations', the forerunners of trade unions. They did this quite simply because collective organization was the only means by which they could protect themselves from the capitalist employers' attempts to cheapen their labour by paying lower wages or employing less skilled workers.

The wool-combers of the clothing industry in the south-west were one of the first to organize themselves in this way. In 1700 the Tiverton wool-combers formed a 'friendly society', which tried to establish a minimum wage and prevent clothiers employing non-members. They engaged in violent disputes with employers who wanted to import already combed wool from Ireland, an early example of the now familiar strategy of exploiting cheaper labour abroad. The wool-combers responded by burning Irish wool, and attacking the houses of clothiers, attacks on property that resulted in pitched battles with the local constabulary.

It was also in 18th-century Britain that typically capitalist ways of thinking about the economic basis of society were first put forward. The merits of the division of labour, competition, the free operation of the market, and production for profit were clearly laid out by Adam Smith. The key thinkers of this time were examining the mechanisms and principles of the capitalist economy that they saw emerging all around them. Their ideas were then criticized but incorporated, with a rather different ideological spin, in Karl Marx's 19th-century analysis of the dynamics of capitalism.

Why had capitalist production become so extensive in 18th-century Britain? One possible explanation lies in the prior growth of merchant capitalism. As we saw in the first chapter, merchant capitalism, particularly in the shape of the East India Company, developed strongly in the 17th century. Once capital had been accumulated in this and other trading ventures, it could be invested in production. Furthermore, international trade enabled the growth of worldwide markets for the goods produced by capitalist industry and in the 19th century the Lancashire cotton industry became largely dependent on the Indian market. Merchant capitalism also created new ways of investing and trading in company shares.

Merchant capitalism was not, however, as closely linked to capitalist production as these arguments would lead one to suppose. It was domestic rather than overseas demand that lay behind the growth of production in the 18th century. Furthermore, as we saw in Chapter 1, those organizing international trading ventures were not, in any case, concerned with reducing the costs of production so much as making money out of the huge differences between the prices paid for goods in the East and the prices at which they could be sold in Europe; they were more interested in manipulating markets than organizing labour. If they wished to invest their capital in other ways, they were more likely to lend it at a good rate of interest to governments, particularly to rulers seeking to finance their frequent wars.

The origins of capitalist *production* in Britain are to be found less in merchant capitalism than in the earlier growth of production, consumption, and markets in 16th-century England. Indeed, the appearance of large enterprises, in, for example, coal mining, has led some to argue that an industrial revolution was already occurring in the 16th century. Most production at this time was, however, small-scale and carried out on a workshop or household basis, hardly industrial in the modern sense of the word. But there was, nonetheless, a remarkable growth in the manufacture of clothing and ordinary household goods, such as buttons and ribbons, pins and nails, salt, starch and soap, tobacco pipes, knives and tools, locks, pots and pans, tiles and bricks. Wage labour was becoming increasingly common and over half the households in 16th-century England were at least partly dependent on wage labour. This meant that people increasingly had money to buy such goods and market relationships were becoming more important in their daily lives. Uniquely in Europe, a national market based on traders operating out of London had already emerged at this time.

With the growth of wage labour came the first stirrings of class organization. We saw above that in the 18th century craft workers were becoming extensively organized in 'combinations'. The very beginnings of worker organization can, however, be found considerably before this. 'Journeymen's societies' were well established in 16th-century Britain and can be traced back to the 14th. Journeymen, literally 'day-workers', were employed by a master for a short period of time. They varied in skill but were commonly craftsmen who had completed an apprenticeship but not yet acquired sufficient skill and experience to qualify as a master. Increasingly masters tried to keep them as cheap labour by obstructing their qualification as masters and excluding them from the guild organizations that controlled the crafts. The journeymen's response was organization, to defend their status and bargain collectively for improvements in wages and working conditions. Although there was still much that was medieval in the ritual activities of their associations, they also used quite modern weapons. In Coventry in 1424 the journeymen in the clothing trade went on strike for higher wages and the town authorities had to intervene to bring about a settlement. Thus, at this early time, craftsmen were already becoming divided into an employing and a labouring class that were in conflict with each other.

Little capital was at this stage involved in most craft production, but in some trades, notably clothing, a new form of production, the 'putting-out system', was coming into existence. In the case of clothing, merchants used their capital to buy wool and put this out to spinners and weavers, before collecting the cloth, distributing it to other crafts for finishing off, and finally selling it. Although this system was organized by merchants, they were much closer than those engaged in international trading ventures to the production process. They were, indeed, commonly craftsmen by origin.

This was a clear and important step on the road to capitalist production. It was not capitalist production proper, for the owner of the capital owned the raw material and the product but did not own the whole of the means of production. Weavers, for example, generally worked at home on their own looms. Production was dispersed through many small units and the merchant did not control the production process or directly supervise the worker. However, in later forms of this system weavers might rent their looms from their capitalist employer, or rent workplaces in workshops owned by the employer, who thereby acquired greater control over them. The putting-out system shaded into the modern factory, though it also persisted alongside it and in the textiles industry still does, for in this industry finishing-off work is still commonly put out to home workers.

Thus, we can trace the origins of capitalist production a long way back, to the 16th century and earlier. What was it about British society that accounts for these early tendencies towards capitalism? Arguably, it was changes in the social relationships of the countryside.

Feudal lords had lived off their rights to produce, labour, or money payments from an unfree peasantry that was tied to the land, but in the 15th century market relationships were beginning to supersede feudal ones. Lords were becoming landowners, who lived off the rent paid by tenant farmers, who competed in a market for these tenancies. The land was worked increasingly by wage labour and was also becoming property that could be bought and sold.

The enclosure movement, which began in the late 15th century and continued intermittently into the 19th, symbolizes these changes in land ownership. This movement fenced off land, sometimes turning what had been common land available to all into private property, and forcing off the land local people who had relied on their right to exploit common land. Sometimes enclosure simply reorganized the traditionally scattered parcels of land held by particular individuals into single, more easily managed, units. The outcome was the division of land into distinct blocks owned by particular individuals. Thus, enclosure cut through complex medieval patterns of land usage and turned land into marketable property.

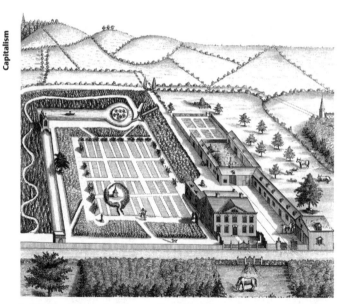

4. The landscape of enclosure: the mid-18th-century estate of David Wells at Burbage in Leicestershire, showing a model farm surrounded by enclosed fields

A market-oriented agriculture contributed to the development of capitalist production in crucial ways. Competition between farmers resulted in innovation and a greater productivity that enabled them to provide food for a growing non-agricultural population. The farmers who marketed their produce, and their waged agricultural workers, had money to spend on consumer goods. Greater agricultural efficiency released labour for employment in making these goods, which were, indeed, produced increasingly in the rural areas where new centres of production were emerging.

Why did market relationships replace feudal ones? One commonly argued reason for the decline of feudal relationships was the impact of the Black Death. In 15th-century England the feudal lords' ability to enforce their rights and control the movement of a subject peasantry had collapsed, largely as a consequence of this disease. The Black Death had reduced the population by around a third in the mid-14th century and empowered a now much smaller agricultural labour force to resist lords' attempts to enforce their rights. Since labour was scarce, peasants could flee oppressive lords and find employment elsewhere. The Black Death was, however, a European phenomenon, which did not have the same consequences everywhere, and cannot itself explain the earlier decline of feudalism in Britain.

So, why did feudalism decline earlier in Britain? Arguably, because it had been less solidly established here. In feudal societies judicial and military authority were dispersed to local lords. They used the power that this decentralization of right and might gave them to subordinate and exploit the peasantry. England had, however, been a relatively unified, orderly, and cohesive monarchy since the Norman conquest in 1066. By the 16th century, under the Tudors, it had become the least feudal and the most unified and centralized of European states. The English ruling class had therefore been less able than its continental counterparts to use its local military power to extract a surplus from the peasantry. It relied more on the economic mechanisms provided by landownership, rent, and wage labour. A relatively unified state also facilitated the emergence of a national market.

So, in seeking an answer to the question – Why was Britain the first capitalist society? – we end up in 1066. But this is not to suggest that the arrow in the eye of King Harold caused capitalism to develop in Britain! It is rather that the consequences of the Norman conquest eventually produced a society more favourable than other European societies to the emergence of a fully fledged capitalism.

Capitalism in Europe

Although Britain was the first society in which production in general became capitalist, there are plentiful examples of the emergence of capitalism elsewhere in Europe. Indeed, the techniques of capitalist organization were at times much more advanced in other European societies.

Capitalist production already had a long history in Europe. The putting-out system seems to have originated in either Flanders or Italy, and had become widespread in 14th- and 15th-century Germany. In Flanders it was initially organized by master weaver-drapers who required little capital for their operations, but by the 13th century the growth there of a luxury cloth trade, with a more complex production process, led to the emergence of 'merchant-entrepreneurs' employing large amounts of capital. This industry imported English wool. The commercialization of agriculture in England was therefore linked to capitalist cloth production in Flanders, clear proof of the need to treat capitalism as European in character.

Merchant capital also became heavily involved in continental mining operations. At the end of the 15th century, merchant capitalists reorganized mining in northern and central Europe. After deposits close to the surface had been exhausted, deep mining, whether of copper, gold, silver, or lead, required large amounts of capital and this provided an opportunity for merchants, such as the Fuggers of Augsburg, to move in and take control of production. The Fuggers had made their fortune from trade and loans to the Hapsburg emperors but then increased it further by investing in mining operations in Austria and Hungary. Their Hungarian mine employed hundreds of workers and was highly profitable. It was in the mines of central Europe that the previously independent miners became wage labour, and the word *arbeite*, German for worker, first came into use at this time.

There were also early signs of a movement towards capitalist production in some continental cities. This was particularly evident in the rapidly developing printing industry. Even though most printing works were small, capital was required to buy the presses and pay for wages, paper, and type. Profits depended on keeping the cost of labour down and there were frequent conflicts between print-masters and their workers, who became highly organized in journeymen's associations. There was a big printers' strike in Lyons in 1539, which spread to Paris in 1541, and there were further flare-ups in these cities in 1567 and 1571.

Capitalist production was then developing all over Europe, not just in Britain, but the growth of capitalism should not be seen just from the perspective of production. The early development of the commercial and financial techniques of capitalism occurred outside Britain. Merchant capitalism was more developed in 17th-century Holland than 17th-century Britain, and key innovations in company finance were made by the Dutch East India Company, well before they were adopted by its British counterpart. The Dutch company's capital was made permanent in 1609. Investors now received dividends from a 'joint-stock' company and could no longer withdraw their capital, though they could sell their shares. This innovation gave companies a more permanent and independent existence by enabling them to build up their capital on a long-term basis. It also created a market in shares and it was no accident that a stock exchange was established in Amsterdam at the same time.

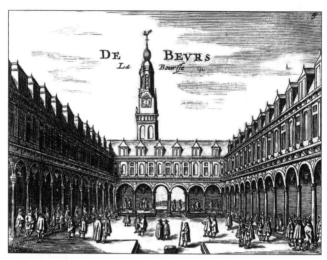

5. The Amsterdam stock exchange, built 1608–13

As we saw in the first section of this chapter, these innovations in merchant capitalism probably had little to do with the growth of capitalist production. The world of the East Indies companies and associated stock markets had little connection with manufacturing. Indeed, the early stages of industrialization in Britain were not financed by investment through joint-stock companies, as the account in Chapter 1 of the rise of M'Connel and Kennedy shows. Most early industrial enterprises were relatively small operations that were funded by families or local loans and then accumulated capital from their profits.

Financial innovations were, however, critical to the growth of the large industrial corporations that in the later 19th century came to dominate capitalist production. If we are to understand the origins of the capitalist world that we live in, an understanding of the growth of large corporations is arguably as important as an understanding of the emergence of capitalist production itself. The great break with the past was not so much the rise of capitalist

28

production, which emerged very gradually through a series of small steps, but the establishment of large, capital-intensive operations organized by great corporations. From this perspective, the financial innovations of merchant capitalism in 17th-century Holland were of immense importance.

These innovations can themselves be traced back from 17th-century Holland to 16th-century Antwerp. There, merchants had developed new ways of financing their trading ventures and spreading risk by drawing on the capital of a wider circle of 'passive' investors. Antwerp was also the centre of a financial revolution based on bills of exchange. These had long existed as a crucial lubricant of trade, for they enabled merchants to pay locally for goods they had bought somewhere else, maybe on the other side of Europe. In the 16th century they were no longer tied to particular trading transactions but became a means of moving money around internationally, thereby enabling the creation of a European capital market. There were also the beginnings of futures trading with the establishment in Antwerp of a commodities market called the 'English House', where contracts to buy English wool were traded without wool ever changing hands.

And we can go back further, for the forerunners of these methods of raising capital and financing trade can be found in the Italian cities, notably Genoa and Venice, of the 12th century. The earliest form of bills of exchange originated in late 12th-century Genoa. The risks of international trade led merchants in the cities to develop new forms of partnership to finance voyages and share risks and profits. By the 14th century advances in book-keeping enabled a much closer control of international trading operations. Innovations of this kind, which figured prominently in early accounts of the history of capitalism, have been sidelined by the more recent emphasis on the development of capitalist production. An understanding of the origins of the corporate and financial capitalism that dominate the contemporary world requires that we put them back in.

These innovations could spread rapidly from the financially and commercially most advanced centres in first Italy, then Flanders, then Holland through the trading and financial networks that criss-crossed Europe, for medieval business was European in its scope. The leading Italian merchant and banking houses had branches in Flanders, England, and France in the 14th century. They even financed the overseas military adventures of the kings of England.

It was also not just business relationships that created such networks but the movement of refugees, particularly in the 16th and 17th centuries. In the second half of the 16th century refugees from Italy and Flanders carried their knowledge, skills, and capital to other countries, to Switzerland, Germany, Holland, and England. The Huguenots, French Protestants with Calvinist beliefs, migrated or were expelled to England and Switzerland and there started new industries, such as lace-making, silk manufacture, and watch-making. Jewish merchants were expelled from Iberia and dispersed all over Europe, some moving to Antwerp and, after their expulsion from there, to Amsterdam.

Its openness to refugees contributed significantly to the development of capitalist production in England. In a discussion of England's economic rise that resonates interestingly with today's debate on immigration, Carlo Cipolla has argued that the economic contribution of refugees has been neglected and comments on the 'extraordinary cultural receptiveness' of Elizabethan England. Indeed, deliberate efforts were made at this time to revive declining clothing industries by bringing in from France and Flanders refugee craftsmen familiar with the latest techniques and products. It was not only the textiles industry that benefited, for new techniques in glass-making, paper-making, and iron-working were also brought in by refugees.

Refugee movements were generated by the religious intolerance and wars of religion that followed the Reformation and

Counter-Reformation, though it was not only for religious reasons that people migrated. The economic disruption caused by warfare and military occupation was another major reason for the exodus from Flanders to Holland. It is also not easy to distinguish economic refugees from refugees of conscience and belief, as in today's world. The areas the refugees left were broadly speaking those that were economically stagnant or in decline and those where they settled were in the forefront of economic development. Economic leadership shifted from Italy to Germany and Flanders, then to Holland, and only later to Britain. Although, as we have seen, both consumption and production had been growing steadily in Britain for centuries, it was not until the 18th century that Britain overtook Holland to become the leading capitalist country in Europe.

Changes in economic leadership could result from shifts in trade, the impact of war, or political and religious change, but they were, as in our own day, partly the result of international competition and the self-undermining consequences of success. Thus, Italian economic decline in the 16th century resulted partly from the shift of trade from the Mediterranean to the Atlantic but was also the result of competition from lower-cost producers in northern Europe. The Italian cities had provided an environment in which crafts could flourish and make high-quality goods, but wages had risen, while the guilds and their regulations prevented innovation. Local attempts to stamp out lower-cost production in rural areas only made the situation worse. The less developed countries of northern Europe, like some less developed Third World countries today, could out-compete the established centres of production.

Thus, while one may reasonably ask why Britain was the first country in which production became capitalist, it is quite wrong to seek the origins of capitalism solely in Britain. This is partly because crucial features of capitalist organization originated outside Britain. It is above all, however, because distinct national capitalisms did not exist at the time when capitalism was emerging. Business networks were European, merchants and workers moved around between countries, and different parts of Europe led the development of capitalism at different times.

Why Europe?

What was it that made Europe the birth-place of capitalism? Virtually every distinctive feature of European society has been advanced by someone as *the* explanation of the emergence of capitalism in Europe.

One possible answer lies in Europe's cities. There has already been much reference in this chapter to the role of cities in the development of capitalism. The Italian cities, then Bruges, Antwerp, Amsterdam, and London, were the source of key innovations in financial and commercial techniques. One of the distinctive features of European society was the emergence in Italy, Flanders, and Germany of networks of relatively independent city-states where commercial and financial, rather than landed, interests ruled.

Cities played an indispensable role, but there are problems with making them *the* explanation of the emergence of capitalism in Europe. There was certainly a period between the 11th and 13th centuries when cities became increasingly independent, but in the centuries that followed they lost much of their autonomy, first to resurgent feudal rulers and then to the nation-state. Also, capitalist production developed more strongly in the countryside than the city, for the guilds in the cities obstructed the ruthless capitalist pursuit of new methods and cheaper labour. Furthermore, as argued in the first part of this chapter, in Britain at least changes in agriculture were crucial to the growth of capitalist production.

Perhaps the answer lies in feudalism itself. The relationship between feudalism and capitalism is intriguing and paradoxical. In many ways feudalism appears quite opposite in character to capitalism. Under feudalism, power and wealth were linked to the control of land not the ownership of capital. Production was not for the market but for consumption by the producer and the lord, who used physical rather than economic coercion to extract the surplus from the producer. There was no 'free' wage labour, for agricultural labour was tied to the land. How could such a society give rise to capitalism?

Although feudal societies have been viewed as reservoirs of anti-capitalist conservatism, they were in many ways flexible and dynamic. Such key features of capitalism as markets and wage labour could emerge within feudal society, and more easily than in either slave-based societies, such as ancient Rome, or the self-sufficient peasantries found in much of the rest of the world. Under feudalism producers had, on the one hand, some degree of freedom, because, unlike slaves, they had limited and specified obligations to their lord. On the other hand, unlike independent and self-sufficient peasants, they were forced to produce a surplus.

A transition to a market economy could also be made relatively easily. Peasants' obligations to provide labour services or produce for the lord could be replaced by money payments, which in turn meant that peasants had to earn money through wage labour or the sale of produce in markets. Lords themselves stimulated trade and manufacturing by spending their ill-gotten gains on luxury products. The class conflict inherent in feudalism could also contribute to this transition, for lords were constantly devising new ways of extracting money from the peasantry, who fought back by exploiting labour shortages to free themselves from feudal obligations and obtain wages in exchange for their labour.

One must add that feudalism did not inevitably shift into capitalism in this way. It did so in Western Europe but not in Eastern Europe, where landowners actually increased the feudal exploitation of the peasantry in the 16th century, in order to make more money from the export of grain to the cities of Western Europe. Thus, the economic development of Western Europe for a time at least intensified feudalism elsewhere. Feudalism had the *potential* to evolve into capitalism but whether it did so or not depended on other factors. In a well-known contribution to the debate on this question, Robert Brenner has argued that the peasants' capacity to organize against their feudal lords and free themselves from feudal bonds was here critical. In the West lords had less control of villages than they had in the East.

Another approach starts from the multi-state political structure of Europe. After the collapse of Rome no ruler was able to establish imperial control over the whole of Europe, though many tried. Some have explained this failure by reference to the ethnic diversity stemming from the multiple barbarian invasions that destroyed Rome. The inability to construct successor empires resulted also from the feudal structure of medieval monarchies. The military and financial weakness of feudal rulers dependent on the military service of unreliable followers and unable to mobilize sufficient resources doomed their imperial ventures to failure. The absence of a Europe-wide empire and feudalism were in this case two sides of the same coin, and we return to feudalism by another route.

But why was the multi-state structure so conducive to the rise of capitalism? The argument here is in part a negative one, for it is claimed that imperial bureaucracies inhibit capitalist dynamism through their taxes, their regulations, and their general subordination of economic development to political stability. There is also the positive point that Europe did not fall into anarchy, for kingdoms were constructed that provided the minimal degree of order necessary for economic development.

The multi-state character of Europe also made it possible for entrepreneurs to move from countries where the economic environment was deteriorating to those providing more favourable conditions for enterprise. Thus, the stifling effects of the rise of the Counter-Reformation state in Italy and Flanders did not halt the development of capitalism because people could move to places where the political regime was less bureaucratic and more tolerant.

As we saw earlier, one of the striking features of the development of capitalism in Europe was the periodic movement of its leading edge from one country to another. As conditions deteriorated in one area, entrepreneurs could find pastures new somewhere else.

Perhaps, however, it was distinctive ideas rather than distinctive structures that resulted in the development of capitalism in Europe. Religious beliefs motivate people, give their actions meaning, and regulate their behaviour through norms that specify how they should live and what they are allowed to do. There is certainly no doubt that powerful religious institutions penetrated into every corner of people's lives in medieval Europe. Were there connections between Christianity and the development of capitalism?

The best-known connection is that made by Max Weber between the 'Protestant ethic' and the 'spirit of capitalism'. Weber was not, it should be noted, arguing that Protestantism caused capitalism but rather that it provided a set of ideas that motivated people to behave in capitalist ways. Protestant beliefs, especially those of the Calvinists (or Puritans, as they were called in Britain), drove people to lead an abstemious life, to save rather than spend, and therefore resulted in the accumulation of capital. Protestants also believed that God should be served not by a religious withdrawal from life but through the proper conduct of the occupation that God had called them to perform. Protestantism brought the religious discipline of the monastery into everyday economic activity and Weber quotes a 16th-century Protestant theologian declaring that 'you think you have escaped from the monastery, but everyone must now be a monk throughout his life'.

This puritan work ethic certainly left its imprint on the attitudes towards work and money typically found in the capitalist societies of northern Europe and North America but, as an explanation of the emergence of capitalism, it has been found wanting. Plentiful examples of Calvinist entrepreneurs can be found, and there was greater economic growth in countries where Calvinism had taken root, but there is not enough evidence that it was Calvinist *beliefs* that were crucial to the emergence of capitalism. Indeed, Henry Kamen has convincingly argued that it was not the religious beliefs of Protestant entrepreneurs but their refugee status that accounted for the apparent relationship between Calvinism and capitalism.

Similarly, Trevor-Roper argued that the Counter-Reformation state drove entrepreneurs out of Catholic areas, notably Italy and Flanders, which had previously been the leading economic centres, into the Calvinist countries of northern Europe. This was partly due to a new religious intolerance, which forced out not only Protestants but also Jews and non-fanatical Catholics with broadly humanistic beliefs, of the kind typically held by Catholic entrepreneurs. It was also because the bureaucracy and high taxation of the Counter-Reformation state were inimical to entrepreneurial activity. Some of the refugees were Calvinist by belief but others became Calvinist by convenience because they ended up in areas where Calvinism was the local religion.

The other side to the debate around the religious origins of capitalism in Europe is the claim that the religions of other civilizations inhibited the emergence of capitalism there. Confucianist China provides an interesting case in point. Its advanced civilization was able to produce many important innovations, inventing paper and gunpowder, but these did not became the basis of an industrial capitalism. Confucianist beliefs in the orderliness of both the natural and social worlds arguably encouraged social stability rather than the dynamism characteristic of capitalism. Michio Morishima has, however, argued that it was the Japanese variant of Confucianism that was largely responsible for the development of a successful capitalism in Japan. The problem with arguments from religion is that religious beliefs can be and are interpreted in so many different ways that religious texts do not themselves explain very much at all.

China was also the opposite of Europe in other respects. It was a bureaucratic empire that lacked the feudal decentralization, autonomous cities, and multi-state competitiveness characteristic of Europe. We cannot therefore isolate the effect of religious differences from other differences that plausibly account for the emergence of capitalism in Europe rather than China.

Rather than expecting that other advanced civilizations would generate capitalism, there are, in any case, good reasons why they did not. Most advanced civilizations were dominated by a single ruling group that used military or religious, rather than economic, coercion to scoop off the surplus from those who produced crops and goods. This surplus was then used for territorial expansion, the maintenance of military power, and projects and displays that enhanced prestige. Some form of bureaucratic apparatus was constructed to tax, regulate, and subordinate the population. Individuals certainly accumulated exceptional wealth and possessions in these societies, but through their connections with the state rather than purely economic activity. There were, in other words, easier ways to become rich and powerful than through the accumulation of capital and the management of labour.

The absence in Europe of a single, cohesive, and totally dominant elite of this kind is the common factor that brings together the various explanations we have been considering. Post-Roman Europe was characterized by political fragmentation, dynastic competition, urban autonomy, and a continual struggle between rulers and ruled. Money could certainly be made through connections with rulers, but states were unstable, rulers were unreliable, and coercion was met with resistance. In these circumstances economic activity could become a more attractive means of acquiring, increasing, and maintaining wealth. The economic mechanisms of market transactions, capital accumulation, and wage labour gradually replaced bureaucratic and feudal means of building it up. The unique structural features of European society provided the conditions in which the machinery of capitalism could emerge and flourish.

Chapter 3
How did we get here?

Capitalism transformed the world but has itself been transformed. We are now in a quite distinct era in its development, one that began in the latest transformation during the 1970s and 1980s. To understand where we are now, we do need, however, to set this new era in historical context. Thatcherism, which embodied its central ideas, set out to reverse many of the tendencies of the previous hundred years and restore the values and vigour of capitalism in the Victorian age.

This chapter examines the development of industrial capitalism by dividing it into three stages. These stages and the labels given to them should not be taken too seriously. They are simply a convenient way of bringing out the distinctive character of different periods and the interconnections between their main features. The stages are outlined with reference to British history, for Britain produced the first industrial capitalism and has been the main source of the key ideas and institutions of capitalist society. The next chapter considers international differences in the development of capitalism.

Anarchic capitalism

This was the stage in the 18th and early 19th centuries when industrial capitalism made its breakthrough. It was anarchic because the activities of capitalist entrepreneurs were relatively unchecked either by organized labour or the state. Small factories and workshops engaged in intense competition with each other, while labour was mobile, pouring into and building the new industrial cities, and constructing the canals, roads, and railways that made possible the mass transportation of goods and people.

As Chapter 2 showed, craftsmen had been trying to organize themselves into associations that would give them some collective power since the earliest days of capitalist production. Employer hostility, intensified by competitive pressures, together with unstable employment and the small size of most units of production, made it very hard for workers to organize but did not stop them trying. In the early 19th century there were numerous and increasingly ambitious attempts to form general unions of all workers. In 1830 the National Association for the Protection of Labour was founded and in 1834 the Grand National Consolidated Union, though neither lasted long. At this time the only unions that could survive were those of skilled workers, who were able to control entry to their craft and were not easily replaceable.

The state did begin to regulate the conditions of factory work. Attempts to limit the number of hours that children could work can be traced back into the 18th century and had their first success in the Health and Morals of Apprentices Act of 1802, though it was not until the 1833 Factory Act that the first effective legislation to do this was passed. While some reformers were motivated by humanitarian concerns, this legislation was not simply directed against exploitation, for there was also much concern with the moral welfare of the women and children employed in the factories and the maintenance of traditional family relationships. The frequently told story of increasing factory regulation gives, anyway, a somewhat misleading picture of the state's involvement in the economy at this time, for important aspects of economic life were being deregulated.

The state machinery set up in the 16th century to regulate apprenticeships, wage rates, and food prices was abolished by 1815. The freeing of international trade took longer but was achieved by the 1860s. The key step in this was the ending of import duties on corn in 1846. Deregulation was in the interests of industrialists, who wanted the freedom to develop their activities without state interference. They wanted wage rates to be set by the labour market not by the state. They also wanted free trade, in part to assist exports but also because imports of cheap food would allow them to pay lower wages.

Deregulation was in tune with the rise at this time of liberal beliefs in the freedom of the individual and the free operation of the market but did not mean that the state totally withdrew. Indeed, the very reverse was the case, for market forces could operate freely only within an orderly society, which required a strengthening of the state at a time when industrial capitalism was generating great disorder. Strikes, rioting, machine-breaking, and crimes against property were threatening both production and order, while trade unions and radical political movements directly challenged the capitalist employer and the state. The military were deployed to quell riots and demonstrations, sometimes with considerable violence.

State welfare hardly existed at this time. The rising number of poor people without means of support did become a cause of increasing concern. This was not, however, because of a concern for their welfare but rather because of a fear that they would become a burden on the local community. They had to be forced to work, and in 1834 the Poor Law Amendment Act introduced a new system of relief to do just that. The existing practice of 'outdoor relief' was abolished and a system of indoor relief created. Only those who entered a 'workhouse' would be given support. Conditions there would be made worse than those experienced by the poorest paid worker, so that only those unable to work would enter. This law generated enormous hostility amongst the poor, and in practice the old system of outdoor relief largely continued, but the 1834 law illustrates well the attitude of the state to poverty during the period of anarchic capitalism.

Competitive small-scale manufacturing, weak labour organization, economic deregulation, a strong state, and minimal state welfare were the mutually reinforcing features of this stage in the development of capitalism. Liberal beliefs in the freedom of the individual were particularly characteristic of this period but not just of historical significance. Liberalism persisted as a powerful set of ideas, which later resurfaced in the 'neo-liberal' guise of the beliefs and policies that have been so influential during the most recent stage of capitalist development.

Managed capitalism

During the next stage in the development of capitalism, which began in the second half of the 19th century and came to its peak in the 1970s, competition and market regulation declined as both sides of industry became more organized and as state management and control increased. International conflict also played its part in this, as governments both sought to protect national economies from a growing international competition and more effectively manage and mobilize their resources against their enemies.

Class organization was one of the main driving forces behind the developments of this next stage. More stable economic growth after the middle of the 19th century, the emergence of larger units of production, and the construction of stronger union organizations produced the conditions in which a national labour movement could at last emerge and survive. Employers too became more organized. Employers' associations were establishing themselves in the second half of the 19th century, as employers banded together at industry level, partly in order to counter the growing industrial power of the unions

6. The Cyclops steelworks in Sheffield, 1853: large units concentrated production and facilitated the organization of labour

but also to reduce the uncertainties generated by unregulated competition.

The main way in which employers reduced uncertainty was not, however, through association but through concentration. The simplest way of dealing with the competition was to buy it up or merge with it. In Britain this process got strongly under way towards the end of the 19th century and there was a further wave of mergers in the 1920s, which resulted in the 1926 creation of ICI (Imperial Chemical Industries) out of four chemical companies that were themselves the products of earlier mergers. Increasing concentration has always been one of the main tendencies in capitalist organization and shows little sign of ceasing.

As corporate units became larger, the management function grew and with it managerial occupations and associations. Some now claimed that a 'managerial revolution' was changing the character of capitalist industrialism. They argued that the growth of management, together with the spread of share ownership to many small and powerless owners, meant that managers rather than shareholders now controlled corporations. Instead of seeking simply to maximize profits, managers took account of the interests of all with a stake in the company. Plausible as it was, this notion of a 'managerial revolution' overstated the power of managers, for owners were still ultimately in control and profitability remained the 'bottom line', but industrial production was undoubtedly a much more managed process than it had been before. Indeed, Alfred Chandler has argued convincingly that the 20th-century supremacy of the American corporation was due to the 'organizational capabilities' of American management. This was one sense in which capitalism had become increasingly 'managed'.

It also became more managed in other ways, as governments responded to class organization by becoming more involved in the management of class relationships. The state shifted from the repression of working class discontent to its management through incorporation, that is through the inclusion and representation of the working class. In the political arena, incorporation took the form of extending the right to vote, most notably in 1867, and the subsequent competition for working class votes between the existing political parties, which delayed the emergence of the Labour Party into the 20th century. This was not founded until 1906, long after comparable parties had been established in other European countries. In the industrial arena, the unions were given some legislative protection during the 1870s, though the employers still took occasional action against them through the courts, until the Trade Disputes Act of 1906 provided them with immunity from civil actions.

The state also increasingly took responsibility for people's welfare. This process began with public health measures in the mid-19th century, but it was not until the decade before the First World War that the foundations of the modern welfare state were laid with the provision of state pensions, of unemployment, disability, and maternity benefits, and of sick pay and free medical treatment by general practitioners. In the 1940s the construction of the welfare state was completed with the provision of free secondary education, the founding of the National Health Service, and the extension of benefits to provide a universal safety-net. Employment is crucial to welfare and the experience of the 1930s depression made the maintenance of 'full employment' one of the highest priorities of postwar governments.

Not only were education and health taken out of the market-place but also other important industries and services. This process started locally with the so-called 'municipal socialism' of the last quarter of the 19th century, which took gas and water supply into public ownership and provided publicly owned city transport. The public provision of housing began with the 1890 law that gave councils the power to build houses. The taking of telephone companies into public ownership began in 1892. Then in the 20th century electricity generation, broadcasting, civil aviation, the railways, coal mining, and many other industries too numerous to list here were created or taken over by the state. Much of this 'nationalization' was motivated not by socialist beliefs in the merits of public ownership but by nationalist concerns with the public ownership of key services and the inefficiency of fragmented or backward industries, which had failed to modernize themselves.

The political incorporation of the working class, the rise of the Labour Party, and socialist ideas evidently played an important part in all this, but it was also driven by international conflict. The breakthrough in the development of state welfare came during the decade before the First World War and reflected not only the political incorporation of the working class but also concerns with the poor physical condition of British soldiers during the Boer War and an awareness of the superior development of state welfare in imperial Germany. The First World War then led to a huge extension of state control over the economy and, although much of this was dismantled afterwards, it did establish important precedents for the future expansion of state ownership. The First World War also boosted class organization, with both the unions and the employers for the first time developing centralized national organizations, in order to influence a government becoming heavily involved in economic management.

The rivalries between empires which lay behind much of the international conflict of the first half of the 20th century drove forward many of the features of managed capitalism, but this was not the only relationship between empires and managed capitalism. As international competition increased after industrial capitalism spread from Britain to other countries, free trade came to be eventually displaced by a protectionism that reached its peak in the 1930s. Markets could be protected, and the supply of cheap raw materials maintained, by constructing an empire and fencing it off from competitor nations. This protection also made it possible for employers to arrive at compromises with the unions that could not have been sustained in the face of increasing competition from countries with higher productivity or lower wages.

Two important qualifications must be made to this argument. Firstly, it is not being argued that empires were constructed solely for economic reasons but rather that, particularly in the British case, they enabled the development of a managed capitalism based on class organization and class compromise. Secondly, by empire is not meant only the colonial territories under imperial government but also those parts of the world dominated by British corporate and financial interests. Britain actually benefited economically more from its investments in Latin American countries that were not colonies but were controlled by British financial interests.

In the quarter century or so after the Second World War managed capitalism reached its fullest extent. It was in the 1940s that a welfare state was fully established and the last big burst of nationalization occurred, though some ailing companies were still being taken into public ownership in the 1970s. Public sector housing expanded and at its peak in 1979 a remarkable third of British households were in the public sector. The governments of the 1960s and 1970s tried to regulate prices and incomes through deals with the unions and employers that offered them some influence over government policy in exchange for cooperation in its implementation. Governments also tried to pursue countercyclical policies that would maintain employment levels. Equality issues were politically prominent, particularly in relation to education, taxation, and welfare.

The evident deficiencies and intense conflicts of anarchic capitalism had generated the contrasting organizations, institutions, and ideologies of a 'managed capitalism', which had a distinctive and coherent character. This second stage was shaped by the growth of large corporations, the development of class organization, corporatist relationships between the state and class organizations, state intervention and regulation, state welfare, and the extension of public ownership, which were inter-related and mutually reinforcing processes. What they all had in common was a reduction in the significance of market relationships in people's lives, reflecting a general reaction against the dehumanizing impact of the market forces that had increasingly shaped the way that people lived during capitalism's breakthrough period. The dynamics of capitalism alone cannot, none the less, account for the development of managed capitalism. It was the national and international context that allowed and assisted these processes to develop, for during this stage capitalism was organized within national empires.

Remarketized capitalism

In the 1960s the welfare state, corporatist relationships between governments and major interest organizations, and extensive public ownership all appeared to be well-established features of British society. The structures and values of managed capitalism had been evolving for at least a century and it looked as though they would continue to develop into the foreseeable future. They certainly had their critics, on the Right and the Left, but were not seriously questioned by mainstream politicians until the end of the decade. Yet, during the 1970s managed capitalism collapsed and in the 1980s a new orthodoxy, centred on the revival of market forces, had imprinted itself on government policy.

Why did managed capitalism collapse? One reason for this was that its corporatist institutions could not in the end be made to work. Government attempts to regulate prices and incomes failed time after time, because the cooperation they required between unions, employers, and the state was either not forthcoming or could not be engineered. When governments adopted more coercive policies, they met a union resistance they could not overcome, a resistance that could prove fatal to the governments themselves. In 1974 the Conservative government's inability to deal with a miners' strike against its incomes policy resulted in electoral defeat, and Labour lost the 1979 election after a 'winter of discontent', when its incomes policy fell apart in a wave of public sector strikes.

It was argued at the time that this failure to make managed capitalism work was a result of the peculiar organizational deficiencies of British industrial relations. This was plausible, given the decentralized and archaic organization of both unions and employers. Their structures had been shaped in the 19th century and had not adapted to economic and social change. Furthermore, corporatist institutions appeared to work smoothly in Sweden, with its more centralized, symmetrical, and functional structures, though Swedish institutions too went into disarray in the 1970s, as the next chapter will show. There was more to the problems of managed capitalism than the archaic character of British institutions.

The real problem was that increasing international competition was putting the old industrial societies under growing pressure, a pressure intensified by the economic crisis of the 1970s, which we examine in Chapter 6. Their employers responded by trying to reduce labour costs, which meant holding down wages, or shedding workers, or increasing productivity, all of which were unpopular with workers and resisted by their unions. As managed capitalism had developed, these unions had increased both their membership and their power so that they were in a strong position to resist changes that they reasonably saw as against the interests of their members.

The managed capitalism of the old industrial societies had enabled them to deal with many of the problems generated by industrial capitalism and arrive at workable compromises between the owners of capital and the organizations of labour. As was noted above, one of the conditions that enabled managed capitalism to develop was, however, the insulation of national economies from international competition. With the decline of empires and the growth of free trade, national insulation was breaking down, international competition was increasing, and the institutions of managed capitalism were put under pressures that they could not handle.

There were also broader changes in values and priorities, which signalled a popular reaction against managed capitalism. There were signs of a growing revolt against higher taxation and a rising dissatisfaction with the take-it-or-leave-it attitudes of public services financed by taxation. These services did not provide the choice or responsiveness that consumers were coming to expect. Even though unemployment was growing in the 1970s, people were becoming more concerned with taxes and prices than jobs. The collectivist concerns with welfare, equality, and employment that were the central values of managed capitalism were giving way to a more individualist focus on freedom and choice.

These changes not only provide part of the explanation for the decline of managed capitalism but also help to account for the direction of its transformation in the 1980s. Managed capitalism had critics on the Left as well as the Right of politics, but in the 1980s it was the right-wing option that triumphed. 'Neo-liberal' beliefs in the freedom of the individual and the free operation of market forces came to dominate ideology and policy. This neo-liberalism sought to reverse the tendencies of managed capitalism and return British society to the vigour of its early capitalist stage. Its main ideas were developed in the 1970s by Keith Joseph, the guru of the New Right, implemented by governments led by Margaret Thatcher in the 1980s, and then adopted by New Labour in the 1990s.

After the Conservatives' election victory in 1979, Keynesianism – the maintenance of high employment through the government management of the economy and public spending – and corporatism were out. There was a clear shift of priorities from the maintenance of employment to the control of inflation. The national organizations of the unions and the employers were no longer consulted about government policy and the representatives of both found themselves removed from state bodies. It was no surprise that union representatives were left out in the cold by a government of the Right, but the Director-General of the CBI, the national employers' organization, was shocked to find that he too was cold-shouldered when he met Margaret Thatcher in 1980. The rejection of corporatist relationships cut both ways.

Market forces were to be revived by 'rolling back the state' in various ways. Welfare expenditure was cut through the restriction of benefit payments, particularly the payment of unemployment benefit, by the replacement of grants with loans, as students know to their cost, and by increases in charges. There was, none the less, no overall reduction of state spending, since rising unemployment resulted in higher social security expenditure. Nor was there an overall reduction in taxation but rather a shift from income tax to indirect taxes, which, it was claimed, at least gave people greater choice, since they did not have to buy the products that carried these taxes.

Public sector industries and services were returned to the market-place through various forms of privatization. Its simplest form was the sale of public companies to private individuals and, according to Yergin and Stanislaw, two-thirds of state-owned industries, amounting to 46 major businesses employing some 900,000 workers, had been sold in this way by 1992. There was also a massive sale of public-sector housing, when the government legislated council tenants' rights to buy the property they lived in. Another form it took was 'compulsory competitive tendering'. This required public-sector agencies to put the services they supplied out to private tender and give the contract to the most competitive bid. In 1983, for example, all district health authorities were required to introduce competitive tendering for the provision of cleaning, laundry, and catering services. An existing 'in-house' provider might win a contract, but to do so it had to behave as if it were a private company.

Other public sector services could not so easily be privatized in these ways. They could, however, be made to behave as though they were competing in a market-place. Thus, the outright privatizing of health and education was not politically possible but the creation of internal markets in health and education forced schools, colleges, and hospitals into competition with each other. At the same time, private alternatives in health and education (and pensions provision too) were subsidized and encouraged. The prison service as a whole was not privatized, but in the 1990s some prisons were placed under private management to generate a competition between private- and public-sector provision.

Market forces were also revived by removing or reducing the state regulation of economic activities. Deregulation too took many forms, such as the removal of restrictions on Sunday trading, the relaxation of planning regulations, and the lighter touch regulation of commercial television. It perhaps had most impact on the financial industry.

This industry had been regulated by the bodies that managed each of its separate areas and maintained the boundaries between them. Building societies and banks, for example, each loaned money but traditionally operated in different markets and did not compete with each other. Boundaries between financial functions, like the barriers between professions, were out of step with the neo-liberal belief in maximizing competition, though this system was breaking down anyway under the pressures of international competition. London and its financial institutions were competing for capital with New York and other financial centres. The removal of international barriers, especially with the abolition of exchange controls in 1979, intensified these competitive pressures by allowing foreign banks a greater freedom to operate in London and British banks a greater freedom to operate abroad. Barings, whose recent story we outlined in Chapter 1, used this new freedom opportunistically and disastrously.

It must, however, be emphasized that although significant

deregulatory changes certainly occurred, there was no overall process of deregulation. As Andrew Gamble has forcefully argued, a free economy requires a strong state. The reviving of market forces actually increased state regulation. There are plentiful examples of this from the Thatcher years.

Privatization alone would not stimulate market competition, if state monopolies were simply turned into private monopolies or private companies were allowed to manipulate markets, so a series of new regulatory 'offices', such as Ofgas, Oftel, and Ofwat, were created to police the gas, telecoms, and water market-places.

In a different way, trade unions were considered to obstruct the free operation of the labour market and were subjected to more legal regulation than they had ever experienced before. They had seen off the 1960s and 1970s attempts by both Labour and Conservative governments to reform them, but in the 1980s they were forced into submission. The legislation that now regulated them was backed by punitive sanctions and defiance could and did lead not only to fines but to a union losing its funds, its buildings, all its assets. The unions took a huge battering from the government in the 1980s, particularly in the carefully planned defeat of the miners' strike in 1984–5. Coal stocks had been built up before the strike was provoked and the police were extensively deployed to frustrate the union's picketing tactics and bring miners before the courts. According to Percy-Smith and Hillyard, there were over 4,000 prosecutions, mainly for public order offences.

The central government also took tighter control of local government, in order to control overall state expenditure and force the privatization of local government services. In education and health, new state apparatuses for improving and auditing their quality, and providing information about their performance, were constructed. There was in fact a greater extension of central state control – over local authorities, education and health, and trade

7. Rolling back: the state uses the police to defeat the miners in 1984

unions – than had ever previously occurred in peace-time Britain and the state was not actually 'rolled back' at all.

That all this was not just the result of Conservative government and reflected a new stage in the development of capitalism is shown by the broad continuation of neo-liberal policies by New Labour. There have admittedly been some departures from the Thatcherite script, as with the introduction of a minimum wage, the granting of recognition rights to the unions, and a partial return of the railways to the public sector. The minimum wage was, however, set at a low level, while most of the legislation regulating union behaviour has been left intact, and privatization has been continued rather than reversed. Labour has indeed explored complex and ingenious ways of extending privatization into new areas through the device of public-private partnerships, which draw private capital and management into public services. Thus, private companies have taken over the management of 'failing' schools and even 'failing' local education authorities.

Labour's plan for the National Health Service (NHS) provides a good illustration of its approach. Although Labour had heavily criticized, and supposedly abolished, the internal market introduced by the Conservatives, market mechanisms were prominent in its 2002 plan for the NHS. Patient choice was at the heart of this plan, which claimed that patients and their doctors would eventually be able to choose when and where patients would be treated, even allowing them to choose private or overseas hospitals. Since funding would follow patients, hospitals would be under pressure to compete for them. There was much emphasis on achieving better performance through decentralization, incentives, and 'payment by results'.

All this reliance on market mechanisms did not, however, mean that the market rather than the state would regulate the NHS. The National Institute for Clinical Excellence would ensure that the most cost-effective treatments were used. National Service

Frameworks would lay down standards of treatment. A 'health super-regulator', called the Commission for Healthcare Audit and Inspection, would monitor performance, grade health-care trusts, and scrutinize complaints. The Commission for Social Care Inspection would regulate nursing and the care of old people. All this was in addition to the hundreds of targets spelled out by the government's National Plan for Health.

The distance travelled by New Labour from the socialist ideas of the past is shown by key changes in its values. There has been a broad shift from collectivism to individualism, as New Labour has distanced itself from its traditional social base, the trade unions. Labour's enthusiastic conversion to consumer choice in education and health demonstrates this individualism well. There has been some redistribution, particularly through measures to reduce child poverty, but the upward 1980s leap of inequalities in income distribution has not been reversed and income inequalities have indeed increased further. Much of the redistributive egalitarianism that sought to use the state to transfer resources from the rich to the poor has been displaced by a more individualist provision of greater opportunities for the poor to realize their potential. Significantly, inequality is now discussed in terms not of differences in wealth or income but of access. As Anthony Giddens has put it 'the new politics defines equality as *inclusion* and inequality as *exclusion*'.

Transformations of capitalism

In this chapter we have examined two transformations in capitalism. What can we learn about capitalism from them?

The first transformation, from anarchic to managed capitalism, showed that it was possible to protect people from at least some of the worst consequences of the operation of market forces. The conditions of work could be regulated and through collective organization workers could limit the power of the employer and negotiate improvements in wages and conditions. Welfare became a matter for the state, which removed key services from the market-place so that they could be provided equally to all citizens. Governments tried to manage the economy by developing cooperation between the state and the organizations of unions and employers. Capitalism could be managed, even if those trying to manage it often got things wrong, sometimes gave in to pressure from the powerful owners of capital, or simply failed to deliver what they had promised.

The fundamental problem faced by managed capitalism was, however, that in restricting and replacing the market provision of goods and services it was weakening the central mechanism of a capitalist economy. When increasing international competition and the economic crisis of the 1970s placed severe strains on the old industrial societies, managed capitalism began to break down. Managed capitalism was also undermined by an increasing individualism that gave greater priority to consumer choice and market provision. There were calls for a return to the values and vitality of earlier times.

In a second transformation market forces were revived, but there was no 'rolling back' of the state, for market mechanisms could only operate in the context of state intervention and regulation. Indeed, the whole notion of an earlier stage in which the market ruled was a myth, for during the time of anarchic capitalism the state had, through the maintenance of order, played a key part in enabling capitalism to function. The latest stage, of remarketized capitalism, has in fact been characterized by a massive increase in state regulation, which has become more extensive than it ever was during the period of managed capitalism.

The new world of remarketized capitalism provides greater choice and more freedom for the individual but also a less secure life, intensified work pressures, and greater inequality. Whether one considers consumer goods, media channels, holiday destinations, or schools, there is no denying the provision of greater choice. Futures have, however, become less secure, particularly in those critical areas of people's lives – employment, housing, and pensions. Insecurity and the weakening of union organization have reduced the capacity of employees to resist the employers' demands for harder and better work, demands driven by increased competition and closer state regulation. The gap has widened between those trapped in low-wage occupations who face insecure futures and those able to exploit the new opportunities to accumulate wealth. As managed capitalism developed, the freedom of the individual was diminished in the name of greater equality, but in a remarketized capitalism, equality and security have been sacrificed to freedom and choice.

There is little sign of this changing in the near future, but it would be wrong to assume that this is the final stage in the development of capitalism. If the market now appears unassailable, so did managed capitalism in its time. If managed capitalism had many weaknesses and deficiencies, so does remarketized capitalism, for inequalities and insecurities create their own inefficencies and pressures for change. Furthermore, as we show in Chapter 6, this new stage in the development of capitalism has itself been dogged by instability and recurrent crises. The remarketizing of capitalism has not solved the problems of capitalist society.

Chapter 4

Is capitalism everywhere the same?

As managed capitalism developed in different societies, it took very different organizational and institutional forms, but in the wake of the 1970s crisis the neo-liberal model of capitalism became intellectually and ideologically dominant. This model seemed to be driving all societies towards a new market-based uniformity. Does this mean that capitalism is becoming everywhere the same? Or have the international differences of managed capitalism persisted and maintained the diversity of capitalist societies? This chapter examines the development and transformation of three very different systems of managed capitalism in Sweden, the United States, and Japan.

Swedish capitalism

Managed capitalism in Sweden probably comes closest of the three to managed capitalism in Britain. Like Britain it has had a strong labour movement, a highly developed welfare state, and minimal state involvement in the industrialization process, though Sweden was rather more successful in developing an efficiently functioning managed capitalism.

The circumstances of Sweden's industrialization were quite different to Britain's. Sweden industrialized later and with only a small domestic market, because of its small population, and without the markets and resources of an overseas empire. Swedish industry was therefore dependent upon exports and had to be highly competitive if it was to survive. Indeed, some have argued that this pressure forced Swedish unions and employers to cooperate and explains the 'labour peace', for which Sweden later became well known.

This view is quite misleading, for there was intense class conflict during the early years of industrial capitalism in Sweden. In 1909 there was a five-month-long general strike that makes the British general strike of 1926, which lasted one whole week, look like a gentlemanly cricket match. The 1909 strike resulted from a steady escalation of conflict, as each side of industry extended its organization in order to outgun the other. Socialists were heavily involved in union organization and in the particular context of Swedish industrialization were able to create a strong and unified organization of the working class. Swedish employers responded by constructing a highly centralized national employers' association, which forced a comparable centralization on the unions. The absence of ethnic and religious divisions and low levels of individualism in a Lutheran society may well have facilitated strong class organization, but conflict was the driving force behind it.

Class cooperation came out of class conflict. The growth of such strong organizations made possible a staunchly corporatist form of managed capitalism, in which its management was substantially delegated to the central organizations. While British governments struggled in the 1950s and 1960s to get the national organizations of the unions and employers to take responsibility for wage restraint, Swedish governments could largely leave this to them. Indeed, Sweden acquired a reputation for 'labour peace' mainly because of the control these powerful organizations exerted over their members. Thus, it was the very intensity of class conflict in Sweden that created the conditions for organized class cooperation and peaceful industrial relations.

A strong and unified labour movement also provided the basis for a long period of Social Democratic government, from 1932 until 1976. This established its reputation through measures to relieve unemployment in the 1930s and an early adoption of Keynesian policies. It later created an advanced and extensive welfare state, based on high and progressive taxation.

State welfare was but one aspect of the collectivist policies of the labour movement. This also strove to reduce inequality through a 'wage solidarity' policy that remarkably compressed wage differentials, with the gap between the average wages of the higher and lower paid halving during the 1960s and 1970s. In the 1970s there was also extensive legislation to protect employees in the workplace and give them a voice in company policy. Such policies were not simply pursued out of ideology. They were part of a Social Democratic strategy to increase the labour movement's organizational and political strength by creating a common interest and identity amongst all employees, working class and middle class.

All this did not mean that Social Democratic Sweden was becoming a non-capitalist society. The labour movement's leadership recognized that welfare depended not just on the strength of socialist ideas and working class organization but also on the operation of a dynamic capitalist economy that could compete internationally and increase the size of the national economic cake. It was one of the central principles of Swedish economic policy that unprofitable companies should be allowed to go bankrupt, so that their resources could be transferred to profitable sectors of the economy. Swedish workers were in this respect rather less protected than British workers by government interventions to bail out failing companies. Furthermore, the union-controlled labour market policy did not protect jobs but assisted workers to become mobile and retrain.

Sweden showed that a Social Democratic welfare capitalism could really work, and this was apparently confirmed by its avoidance of

Thatcherism. Levels of industrial conflict did rise and Sweden too faced economic crises in the 1970s. Indeed, there seemed to be a parallel with Britain as a growing individualism and the shift of politics to the Right resulted in six years of 'bourgeois' government between 1976 and 1982. The Swedish Right was, however, historically divided between three parties that could not cooperate sufficiently to carry through a Thatcherite transformation. The Social Democrats then returned to government and this, together with favourable economic conditions, suggested that the Swedish model had weathered the storm.

This was an illusion, for the corporatist cooperation central to the Swedish model was now in a state of collapse. Centralized organization had generated its own tensions, not only between centre and periphery but between different sections of labour. The inevitable extension of centralized organization to white-collar and public-sector workers, as their occupations grew, produced very powerful organizations and these then engaged in competitive rivalries, which the centralized structure of Swedish bargaining could not contain and, if anything, amplified. The central wage negotiations became longer, more complex, and more conflictual. In the process Swedish employers became thoroughly alienated from the institutions of central cooperation.

They were also alienated by another sequence of changes. In the 1960s workers became discontented with the impact on their jobs and work conditions of Sweden's dynamic capitalism. A submerged labour radicalism resurfaced with demands for greater industrial and economic democracy. This culminated in the ingenious Meidner Plan to transfer gradually the ownership of industry from private capital to union-controlled funds, though only a heavily watered-down version was actually legislated. The Social Democrat leadership was not going to wreck the capitalist engine of Swedish economic growth. Serious damage was done, none the less, to the relationship between the labour movement and the employers.

The *modus vivendi* established in the 1930s between the labour movement and the employers had come to an end. During the 1980s the main employers' organization embarked on a broad counter-attack to reinstall the values of an individualist and capitalist society. There was an employer drive to decentralize and individualize wage bargaining, and in 1990 the employers finally withdrew from the central wage bargaining that had enabled the reduction of wage differentials. Their strategy switched from a corporatist representation of their interests on state bodies to a greater use of political influence and lobbying. Corporatism had been dismantled in Sweden, though by the employers rather than by a bourgeois political party, as in Britain.

A limited remarketizing of Swedish society had already begun as Swedish politics moved in a neo-liberal direction during the later 1980s. Welfare capitalism had generated a large public sector, high public expenditure, a large government deficit, and inflationary wage settlements, which were evidently eroding Swedish competitiveness. Business leaders warned that unless changes were made they would have to move their operations out of Sweden and the leadership of the Social Democratic Party recognized that industry was becoming uncompetitive. Exchange controls were lifted and financial markets deregulated; private capital was brought into state-owned industries; local authority services were operated increasingly on business lines; benefits and public expenditure were cut; taxation became increasingly indirect.

The crunch came in the early 1990s. The economic crisis that had been brewing in the 1980s arrived and GDP fell by 5% during 1991–3, while unemployment soared to levels not seen since the 1930s. The Social Democrats could not cope and were rejected by the electorate in 1991. Three years of 'bourgeois' government led by Sweden's most right-wing party followed. This meant further cuts in benefits and the introduction of more market mechanisms in the delivery of social services. Then when the Social Democrats returned in 1994 they too had to cut welfare expenditure in order to deal with a large government deficit. In the 1980s many had thought that the Swedish case proved that the Social Democratic alternative was still viable, but the early 1990s seemed to show that it was not.

The key issue here is the kind of comparison that is made. If Sweden in the early 21st century is compared with Sweden in the 1960s and 1970s, then there is no doubt that the 'Swedish model' of central cooperation, welfare capitalism, and growing equality has declined. As in other societies, inequality started to increase again during the 1980s. But if contemporary Swedish capitalism is compared with contemporary capitalisms elsewhere, there are considerable and significant differences, some of which are actually increasing.

Central wage agreements no longer exist but their replacement by broad sectoral agreements between employer and union groupings shows that Swedish wage bargaining has remained highly coordinated. Union membership has declined but is still, internationally speaking, exceptionally high, with 81% of employees unionized in early 2003, as compared with around 30% in Britain in recent years. This difference had in fact widened, as union membership declined much faster in Britain than Sweden.

The Swedish welfare state is also still distinctive. The Organization for Economic Cooperation and Development's (OECD's) summary measure of state benefit entitlements shows Britain and Sweden at virtually the same level in 1981, a substantial gap then opening up between them during the 1980s, as benefits were cut in Britain, and largely persisting since then *in spite of* the cuts in Sweden. Duane Swank's review of recent research on the Swedish welfare state concludes that there has not been 'much if any convergence of the Swedish welfare state with its neoliberal counterparts'.

Furthermore, these deviations from the neo-liberal model have been compatible with economic revival and a viable capitalism.

Sweden did go through a severe economic crisis in the early 1990s but has since recovered. Unemployment dropped from the 10%-plus level reached early in the 1990s to a tolerable 4% in 2001. The 2002 OECD Economic Survey of Sweden concluded that 'overall, the economy is performing well'.

So what does the Swedish case tell us about capitalism? It shows that in certain conditions the conflict between employers and unions generated by capitalism can provide the basis for centralized class cooperation and a functioning system of corporatist management and welfare capitalism. It also shows that such a system could not in the end contain the underlying conflicts between capital and labour, and sections of labour, which eventually paralysed it. Increasing international competition and global economic integration made such a high-cost system difficult to maintain. Economic crisis was postponed but could not be avoided, and Sweden had to conform *to some degree* to international neo-liberal tendencies. All this did not mean, however, that the structures and institutions created during the period of managed capitalism disappeared. The revitalizing of Swedish capitalism did not eliminate its collectivist distinctiveness, which remains and is proving perfectly compatible with economic growth.

American capitalism

With its pronounced individualism, American capitalism has been at the opposite end of the ideological and organizational spectrum. Industrialization occurred in a decentralized and individualist society, where there was a widespread belief in success through enterprise and initiative. The absence of an aristocracy and the establishment of political and civil rights by the 18th-century American Revolution had encouraged such beliefs. The growth of industrial capitalism did result in the formation of unions, but these were mainly self-interested organizations of craft workers that were not concerned with class organization or the socialist transformation of society.

In this context the business corporation flourished and produced a corporate rather than corporatist capitalism, in which business corporations rather than class organizations were the dominant actors. The large American domestic market enabled the growth of big corporations and in the late 19th century a greater concentration of ownership occurred than in other industrial societies. At first this took the form of 'horizontal' mergers to give control over markets, as in Rockefeller's construction of Standard Oil. It was, however, the 'vertically' integrated corporation, which built a strong and secure competitive position by bringing together all stages in the production and distribution of a product, that became the dominant form in the 20th century.

America was the home of the 'managerial revolution' theory, discussed briefly in Chapter 3. Although this underestimated the continued power of owners, it has been argued convincingly by Alfred Chandler that the managers of American corporations were distinctively allowed to 'get on with the job' during the period of corporate growth, which largely resulted from their highly developed 'organizational capabilities'. Chandler contrasted American management, with its use of profits to finance investment and growth, with the more personal and traditional ownership of British companies, which were more concerned with dividends to shareholders than long-term investment.

The centrality of the business corporation was paralleled by the distinctive character of American trade unionism. This was predominantly a 'business unionism' concerned not with social transformation or even the collective interests of labour as a whole but with obtaining the best possible contract for union members. This meant not only good wages but also fringe benefits, such as holidays-with-pay, insurance, and health care, particularly after the Second World War. This business unionism reflected not only domination by the business corporation but also the divisions within the American working class. It was the unionism of white, male workers and has been regarded as a deviant form by its class-conscious and socialist European counterparts. The proportion of employees unionized barely topped one-third even at its peak and this was already declining in the 1950s, though the unions were still well able to deliver the goods for those who were their members during the 1950s and 1960s.

As the importance of fringe benefits shows, some of the welfare that in Europe was the province of the state was in America provided by the corporation. Indeed, the term 'welfare capitalism', commonly used to describe the combination of a dynamic capitalism with an advanced welfare state, in America refers to corporate welfare provision. This is not to say that there was no development of state welfare in America, but this only provided a piecemeal safety-net for the poor and welfare was otherwise the responsibility of the corporation or the individual, and was delivered by private services operating through the market-place.

It would also be quite wrong to suppose that individualism and free market ideologies kept the state out of economic life. On the contrary, the monopolistic tendencies of business corporations meant that economic life required regulation, if competition were to be maintained and the interests of consumers protected. An 'anti-trust' movement emerged in the late 19th century and the Sherman Act of 1890 declared illegal any activity or organization 'in restraint of trade or commerce'. This did not stop the growth of powerful corporations, but it did have consequences, notably forcing the break-up of Standard Oil, and it did give rise to a distinctively American apparatus of anti-trust legislation and enforcement. The state had been drawn into economic life not by class conflict, as in Europe, but in defence of competition.

In the 1930s state intervention appeared to take a much more European direction. In response to the Great Depression, Franklin Roosevelt's New Deal legislated ambitious relief and welfare programmes, eventually adopting Keynesian economic policies. It

8. 'Ring-around-a-Roosevelt': his New Deal offspring dance around him

came into considerable conflict with big business over its taxation proposals; its drive to provide, partly through the publicly owned Tennessee Valley Authority, cheap electricity; its continuation of the 'anti-trust' attack on monopolistic tendencies; and its legislation to protect trade unions.

Unions were given the right to organize and bargain collectively, and a National Labour Relations Board was set up to enforce these rights. Union membership tripled between 1933 and 1938, as the Committee for Industrial Organization (CIO) established a more inclusive trade unionism and organized America's mass production industries. Further legislation to regulate wages and hours of work, and protect vulnerable groups, was passed in 1938.

The federal structure of the state, and its fragmenting division of powers between President, Congress, and Supreme Court, gave opponents many opportunities to block and frustrate New Deal measures. Furthermore, although the New Deal created an astonishing range of agencies and programmes, it lacked coherence, at least in comparison with the more ideological programmes developed in Europe. It depended on the commitment and energy of Roosevelt and an army of well-intentioned and highly motivated reformers and administrators, but there was no reformist political party to support it and drive it forward. The Democratic Party, Roosevelt's political base, did ally itself with the unions and supported state welfare programmes but it was not a 'labour party' and contained people hostile to the unions and the New Deal.

The pro-labour legislation of the 1930s was, indeed, at least partly reversed by the Taft-Hartley Act of 1947, which substantially weakened the unions' powers and rights. This was passed by Congress, against the veto of Roosevelt's successor, Harry Truman, demonstrating the weakness of a labour movement without a political arm. The American unions already faced in the 1950s the kinds of restrictions on their behaviour that the British unions did not have to confront until the 1980s.

In other respects, the managed capitalism of the New Deal continued to operate during the 1950s and 1960s. The social security legislation and welfare programmes introduced in the 1930s were extended in the 1950s and 1960s, especially to give free medical care to the poor and the old. As late as the 1970s, during Richard Nixon's presidency, the federal government experimented with the control of prices and incomes. Deficit financing continued, though not simply because Keynesian economics had become the new orthodoxy, for the Second World War and then the Cold War resulted in massive military expenditure. The profitability of substantial sections of industry, and therefore the employment and earnings of labour, depended on state spending. The whole idea of a state-directed industrial policy was anathema in the United States, but, as David Coates has argued, the creation of a military-industrial complex was, in effect, one form of such a policy. Business opposed government interference but accepted government money.

While American industry was in better competitive shape than British industry, it too suffered in the later 1960s and 1970s from inherited rigidities and intensified international competition, especially from Japan. Lower levels of trade unionism, state welfare, and public ownership did mean that there was less pressure to transform the state than in Britain. The United States was half way to Thatcherism already. But there was still half way to go, and the United States too went through a process of transformatory change, albeit at a slower speed, with frequent halts and occasional reversals along the way.

Thus, in the 1980s and 1990s, American society too was remarketized. Keynesianism was abandoned, government expenditure was cut, some industries were deregulated, some services privatized, and state welfare reduced. The 1970s' inflation discredited Keynesian policies. The Reagan administration of the early 1980s then sought to stimulate market forces by cutting both taxes and government expenditure, though vested interests resisted cuts in the latter and the reduction of the budgetary deficit was a slow process. The deregulation of the airlines marked the first break with the New Deal tradition of industrial regulation and was followed by the deregulation of the railways, trucking, telecommunications, and electricity generation. The publicly owned part of the railways, and many state-run local services and prisons, have been privatized. A welfare-to-work programme, which became a model for New Labour in Britain, limited the duration of welfare payments and forced recipients into low-paid work.

As in Britain, these changes were accompanied by the greater exploitation of labour through an intensification of work, declining real wages, and the weakening of unions. Hours of work lengthened and real wages dropped at the rate of 1% a year during the 1980s. Industrial corporations moved their plants south from the 'rust belt' to the 'sun belt' and then Mexico, in search of cheaper labour. Elitist 'business unions' concerned with meeting the immediate needs of their existing members either failed to organize the new labour force or (in Mexico) could not. By 2001 union density had dropped to a very low 13% of the labour force. Inequality increased, with the number living in poverty rising from around 25 million in the 1970s to around 35 million in 2002.

There were equally important changes in management, as the 'managerial revolution' of the early 20th century was reversed. The greater mobility of capital, popular investment in the stock market, and the expansion of the financial services industry increased the importance of a company's market valuation. According to the newly fashionable doctrine of 'shareholder value', the goal of management was no longer to invest in the future or build up a company or balance the needs of its various interests but only to maximize the value of its shares by increasing profits. Managers were given an incentive to do this through stock options which rewarded them for increases in their company's share price. Managers had been to some extent separated from owners by the managerial revolution, but now they increasingly became owners.

From the mid-1980s to the late 1990s, the intensified exploitation of labour and the emphasis on shareholder value raised corporate profits. There was economic growth, but not for long. Much of the growth was associated with an information and communication technology boom that had to come to an end some time. In the later 1990s, when exports weakened, growth was sustained by a surge in domestic consumer demand that was financed by a borrowing spree that could not go on indefinitely. The preoccupation of companies and investors with share prices encouraged a bubble mentality that pushed prices up to levels unjustified by earnings and profits, giving people a false sense of their wealth and then suddenly removing it when the bubble burst. The short-term concern with share prices at the expense of future prospects led to financial scandals at Enron and Worldcom, and in Wall Street, which undermined confidence and discredited the pursuit of shareholder value (see Chapter 6).

Much of the 1990s' confidence in the virtues of the American model has been dissipated and there is considerable uncertainty about the future. Higher state spending, with military and reconstruction expenditure rising in Iraq, together with tax reductions and lower interest rates, may stave off recession and even promote some recovery. Weakening exports, higher state spending, and high domestic consumption have, however, generated a huge international, public, and personal indebtedness, which is storing up problems for the future, as are higher unemployment and rising poverty.

American capitalism has from its beginnings been characterized by strong beliefs in individualism and market forces, but the development of American capitalism, like capitalisms elsewhere, did result in the collective organization of labour, corporate concentration, and extensive state regulation. Managed capitalism in America was importantly different to managed capitalism in Britain and Sweden – collective organization was less extensive, state welfare less universal, anti-trust legislation more developed – but America did, none the less, go through this stage.

The current state of American capitalism reflects its historic distinctiveness, but it is not just the expression of some special character that American capitalism possesses. It is also the result of the remarketizing of American society after the crisis of the 1970s. This remarketizing process met less resistance and fewer obstructions than it did elsewhere and produced strong growth, but also created a bubble that eventually burst, and generated serious economic and social problems. The recent recovery looks fragile and American economic success towards the end of the 20th century may well be leading to a crisis early in the 21st.

Japanese capitalism

Japanese industrial capitalism was managed from its very beginnings. By the middle of the 19th century Japan was a highly commercialized and entrepreneurial society but not yet an industrial one. After the Meiji Restoration, Japan's 19th-century revolution, industrialization was directed by the state as part of a programme to build a strong and independent country that could stand up to the Western empires that were encroaching upon Japan. The individualism and liberalism of the West were attractive to some intellectuals and policy-makers but alien to Japan's new rulers, who were nationalist bureaucrats schooled in the Japanese version of Confucianism.

One of the best-known ways in which the new government tried to industrialize Japan was by setting up model state enterprises but these were not always successful. Some, such as the Yawata Iron and Steel Works, were crucial to the industrialization process, but others were poorly managed and inefficient. Thus, as Frank Tipton has pointed out, the state-owned cotton spinning factories imported water-powered machines with only 2,000 spindles instead of investing in the latest steam-powered machines with 10,000 spindles, which could be operated by relatively unskilled labour. The state-owned enterprises ran into such difficulties that in the 1880s the government privatized those that were not considered of military importance.

Privatization did not, however, mean that Japanese industry now consisted of independent private companies. A distinctive feature of Japan's industrialization was the emergence of the large industrial groupings known as *zaibatsu*. There were four main groups – Mitsubishi, Mitsui, Sumitomo, and Yasuda. They were owned by families, which controlled them through holding companies. Corporate concentration was occurring in all industrial societies but in Japan it took a unique form, for each *zaibatsu* stretched across virtually the whole of Japanese industry and had its own bank and its own trading company to market its products. The *zaibatsu* were closely connected with the state and eventually performed important colonial functions for the government.

The model enterprises were anyway the least important aspect of the state's promotion of economic growth. The government removed the feudal barriers and restrictions that would have inhibited economic development, and created a modern nation-state. Japan became a unified country for the first time and the heavy subsidizing of railways and shipping transformed communications. Shipbuilding too was heavily subsidized and by 1939 Japan's production was second only to Britain's. The state also created a banking system to finance investment and trade, at first experimenting with American-style private banks but then creating a European-type central bank and specialized banks to cater for the needs of the various parts of the economy.

Above all, the state maintained Japan's economic independence. Many foreign experts had been brought in but were then rapidly replaced by home-grown expertise created through new educational institutions. Foreign capital was kept out, until Japan had become a strong independent state. Indeed, it was the peasantry that bore the main cost of Japan's modernization through a land tax that initially provided three-quarters of the government's income. Japan also began to construct an overseas empire that would provide it with protected markets and raw materials.

Japan was the only non-Western society to industrialize successfully in the 19th century. A distinctive managed capitalism had been created, in which the state played a directive role and corporate concentration took the form of industrial groups that stretched across the economy. Another distinctive feature was the weakness of labour organization. Workers did try to organize, with some success during the First World War, when industry boomed and labour was in high demand, but met heavy employer opposition and state repression. State welfare too was undeveloped, in part because employers preferred to introduce company welfare schemes that integrated workers and detached them from the labour movement.

These distinctive features were further developed during the postwar period, when Japan's growth machine really got going and made the Japanese economy the second largest in the world. Chalmers Johnson has pointed out that military defeat actually increased the state's capacity to direct the economy, by removing military interference and *zaibatsu* obstruction. The *zaibatsu* were dismantled but then reconstructed, as the beginning of the Cold War led the American-dominated Occupation Authority to reverse its policy. Mitsubishi, like Krupp in Germany, now became an anti-communist resource rather than a reservoir of fascism. Crucially, the *zaibatsu* were rebuilt under the aegis of the Ministry of Trade and Industry (MITI), the powerhouse of the state's industrial policy, which used its control of trade, currency, and investment to develop the industries of the future.

The reconstructed *zaibatsu* and other similar groupings performed important economic functions. As they stretched across industry, they provided coordination across industrial boundaries, but they also engaged in intense competition, which stimulated productivity and enhanced international competitiveness. They could pursue long-term policies aimed at building market-share, because their reconstruction on the basis of mutual ownership and their finance by the banks relieved them of shareholder pressure for high dividends. This also meant that they were protected from take-overs by foreign capital or corporate raiders. This pattern of ownership was linked to integration within the company, for Japanese companies could look after their employees instead of maximizing the payment of dividends to shareholders.

Union organization grew rapidly during the first years of the Occupation, giving the lie to claims that Japanese unions have been weak for cultural reasons. In January 1946 there were 900,000 union members, but by June 1949 there were over 6.5 million, as compared with the prewar peak membership of 421,000 in 1936. They were at first encouraged as 'democratic' organizations by the Occupation Authority, but this rapid growth, in the context of the policy shift from an anti-fascist to an anti-communist stance, led to a sustained and violent attack on them by both employers and the state. The employer strategy soon became, however, not the destruction of unions as such but their replacement with tame 'enterprise unions'. At the 'battle of Nissan' in 1953 the company, backed by the Japanese Employers' Association and with financial support from the banks, provoked the existing union into a strike, locked out its members, created its own Nissan union, and gave those who joined it their jobs back. Enterprise unions became the norm.

High company employee integration gave Japanese companies the edge that enabled them to out-compete their Western rivals. The company provided the security of lifetime employment, wages that increased with seniority and length of service, welfare services, and often housing. In return employees had to work hard and long, giving up weekends and holidays if required by their company. Other mechanisms of integration were the absence of status distinctions within the company, company uniforms, and the social interaction of workers and managers both at work and leisure. Earnings differentials have been very much lower in Japanese companies than comparable Western ones.

Integration for some was at the expense of others. Contract workers, part-time workers, and women workers, who were largely confined to these categories, did not enjoy the benefits of lifetime employment and all that went with it. This also applied to the small companies subcontracted to carry out much more of the large company's work than in Western industrial societies. These were the shock-absorbers that enabled the large companies to ride out economic fluctuations by turning their labour on and off as required. There was a sharp division in Japan between an integrated elite of permanent employees and a disposable periphery.

A key set of linkages in a highly integrated institutional structure operated through the Japanese welfare system. There was only a rudimentary welfare state, which kept workers highly dependent on company welfare schemes and reinforced their subservience but also encouraged the Japanese to save privately for a 'rainy day'. Individual savings went into a postal savings scheme controlled by MITI, which could then channel them into industries it had marked out for investment.

So, in Japan there is an undeniably successful capitalism very different in character to the others we have examined. While the welfare state has been an integral part of Swedish capitalism, its absence is crucial to the Japanese model. The state's directive role has been particularly distinctive, and led some commentators to call for Western governments to develop comparable industrial policies. Patterns of corporate ownership and bank finance contrast with the stock-market model of the United Kingdom and the United States. Company domination of workers has been more complete in Japan than even the United States, where unions have been more combative. Company welfare too has been more extensive, and Ronald Dore has described Japanese capitalism as a 'welfare capitalism' in yet another application of this label.

Like the other systems of managed capitalism that we have examined, the Japanese one ran into difficulties in the later 1960s and the 1970s, and Japan also came under heavy and steady external pressure to open itself up to trade. This really began after the early 1970s rapprochement between the United States and China changed the American view of Japan, which was now regarded not as a bulwark against East Asian communism but as an industrial competitor that engaged systematically in unfair trade practices. Although Japan found ways of replacing tariff with non-tariff barriers, famously declaring that Raleigh bicycles were unsafe, restrictions on the import of goods and capital were gradually lifted. MITI's instruments of control were dismantled and it had to rely increasingly on 'administrative guidance' through its extensive network of retired bureaucrats with second careers in industry.

Japan did not, however, respond to the problems of the 1970s by abandoning its institutions and plunging down a neo-liberal path. Growth and international competitiveness were sustained by exporting the capital accumulated through growth and setting up operations to exploit cheaper labour abroad, particularly in South-East Asia, but also in Europe, the United States, and Australia. MITI launched a new drive to develop the knowledge-based industries of the future, and Japan soon became the world's leading producer of microchips. So strong was the competitive strength of Japanese industry that the United States continued through the 1980s to run a huge trade deficit with Japan, though Japanese investment in American bonds recycled some of Japan's earnings back to the United States and financed its deficit.

All this changed at the beginning of the 1990s. Share and land prices had reached unsustainable heights and the bubbles burst. A stock-market crash was followed by economic stagnation and higher unemployment. Japan entered a vicious deflationary circle. As unemployment rose and uncertainty about the future increased, people saved more, consumer demand dropped, and growth declined even further. The problem was not so much in export markets, where many Japanese companies were still very successful, but the domestic market. The government has responded with increased public expenditure and lower interest rates but found it difficult to restart the growth machine.

The institutions that had enabled growth began to attract criticism. Lifetime employment was viewed as a 'rigidity' that interfered with the free workings of a labour market and prevented companies shedding labour. Mutual ownership in the industrial groups was criticized for supporting unprofitable companies and preventing a refreshing inflow of capital from abroad. The banks were considered too closely linked with industrial groups and therefore unable to pull the plug on unprofitable companies. Indeed, many banks were themselves in serious trouble because they had loaned so much money to bankrupt speculators and failing companies. Faltering economic growth and the exposure of corrupt links between companies, banks, political parties, and bureaucrats combined to undermine the 'developmental state'. Inside and outside Japan, there were calls for Japan to conform to the market model that, it was claimed, the pressures of globalization in any case made unavoidable.

Japan has therefore come under a growing pressure to allow a greater mobility of capital and deregulate financial markets. Foreign capital has moved into Japan, with some ailing companies being bought by foreign competitors, as in Renault's take-over and rationalization of a failing Nissan. The so-called 'big bang' deregulation of banking and finance announced in 1996 has allowed Japanese capital greater freedom and facilitated the entry of foreign financial interests. Bankruptcies and rationalization followed, as weak institutions lost their protection. The term 'big bang' belied, however, what was in reality a slow and partial process of implementation that was not at all comparable to the 'big bang' in London. There is some acceptance that Japan must adapt but not that it must conform.

Can Japanese institutions be preserved? In his recent examination of these issues, Ronald Dore has chronicled a process of gradual change, with the main Japanese employers' association rethinking lifetime employment; legislative changes to strengthen shareholder power; a movement towards performance-related payment systems; and some liberalizing deregulation. Dore also comments frequently, however, on the superficiality of change, resistance and reaction to it, and the inertia of a system with so many interlocking parts.

9. Carlos Ghosn, the Nissan CEO from Renault, announces the closure of factories, October 1999

What is striking about Japan is in fact its stability, both political and economic. In the early 1990s it looked as though the long-standing domination of Japanese politics by the Liberal Democratic Party (LDP) was breaking down and a political alternative was emerging, but the main opposition party, the Japanese Socialist Party, then entered a coalition with the LDP, which has subsequently maintained its dominant position. The astonishing growth rate of earlier years has not been maintained and Japan has certainly experienced much economic pain in the 1990s, notably higher unemployment, but its current unemployment rate is actually considerably lower than the OECD average. The world's second largest economy has been kept afloat and has not tumbled into depression. If you have experienced massive economic growth and have a high standard of living, stagnation may not be a bad option! This stability may be expected to preserve Japanese institutions.

The pressure to marketize Japanese society may also be lessening. Shareholder capitalism, certainly in its American guise, was riding high in the 1990s but, as indicated earlier, this is currently under something of a cloud after the accountancy scandals at Enron and Worldcom, while, after the bursting of the late 1990s bubble, the American economy appears fragile. Those seeking to resist the liberalizing of the Japanese economy now have ammunition to counter the arguments of those who have been pressing for a liberal transformation of Japan.

Convergence?

We have examined the emergence of three national systems of managed capitalism with distinctive organizations and institutions. In all three, capitalist industrialization generated class organization and class conflict, and attempts by governments to manage the problems of a capitalist society. Each also created its own 'welfare capitalism', though this meant different things in each society.

Although each seemed to have solved the problems of capitalism in its own way, all three faced growing difficulties from the 1970s, in part because of changes in the world economy but in part because of the problems that their distinctive institutions had created. All came under pressure to abandon their practices of managed capitalism and introduce reforms that would allow market forces greater freedom to operate.

Has this led to the decline of national differences? Instead of capitalisms is there now just one all-conquering capitalism? There is plentiful evidence of continued national distinctiveness. Nor does the fact that all three have moved in a similar direction mean that they have converged, in the sense that they are any closer to each other. If three people standing one metre apart each move one metre to the right they are still as far apart as they were before!

It is important to resist the notion of an inevitable convergence, not only because it is untrue but also because it deprives us of choice. In a world where functioning alternatives to capitalism have been eliminated, it is only the alternatives within capitalism that provide choice. This does not mean that one can simply pick whatever capitalism one chooses, for the existing institutions in any one society constrain free choices, but it does mean that people can strive to move their particular capitalism in the direction they think appropriate. The argument that market forces inevitably and increasingly override politics in a capitalist society cannot be sustained, for the comparative study of capitalisms shows that quite different organizational and institutional structures have survived remarketization and are perfectly compatible with functioning market mechanisms.

Chapter 5
Has capitalism gone global?

The words 'global capitalism' have become commonplace and there is much to suggest that capitalism is now organized on a global basis. Huge sums of money are transmitted across the world on a daily basis. Companies no longer produce in one country for export to others but run manufacturing operations in many different countries in distant parts of the world. Markets for goods and services, for capital and labour too, are in many ways global in extent. These are the realities of global capitalism that impact daily on people's lives, but there are also many myths associated with this notion. In this chapter we explore both the realities and the myths.

Global capitalism old and new

A first myth is that global capitalism is something new. Almost as soon as it had come into existence, capitalism spread across the world. The navigators of the 15th and 16th centuries, who piloted the routes from Europe to other continents, were quickly followed by merchant capitalists. The East India companies brought the products of Asia to the consumers of Europe and exported their manufactures in return. The Atlantic trade triangle shipped goods from Europe to Africa, sold slaves from Africa to the Americas and the Caribbean, and took back to Europe the sugar, rum, and cotton they produced.

Travel was, however, slow, intermittent, and hazardous until the communications revolution of the 19th century, which was quite as profound as the one that we have recently been living through. It was not only that steam-powered trains and ships speeded up travel, they also enabled the mass transportation of goods and people across the world, and on a regular and reliable basis independent of the weather. The invention of the telegraph meant that messages no longer had to be carried by people or pigeons, and after the laying of submarine telegraph cables London could communicate with Australia in 4 days rather than the 70 taken by surface mail. The later invention of the telephone for the first time 'destroyed distance' by making possible instant communication across the world.

It was also in the 19th century that an organized global economy came into existence. Its central principle was an international division of labour between a small group of manufacturing nations and the rest of the world, which became a market for their goods and the source of the food and raw materials they could not provide for themselves. Capital moved freely between countries but within the framework provided by the gold standard, which after 1870 increasingly regulated the relationships between national economies. It did this by fixing the value of currencies in relation to gold, until this standard disintegrated under the pressures generated by the 1930s depression.

This global economy was organized within empires that were extensions of the nation-states at their core. These empires took the form not only of colonial territories but also of spheres of influence that divided up areas of the world not under direct colonial control. While Europe first created overseas empires, the United States constructed its own less formal empire in the Pacific and Latin America, and in the last quarter of the 19th century Japan began to follow the European model and acquire its first overseas territories. Under the pressure of international competition and the economic crises of the early 20th century, the world became increasingly divided by imperial boundaries, as each country tried to protect its overseas markets and supplies. After the First World War the movement towards growing global economic integration actually went into reverse.

After the Second World War this imperial framework began to collapse. New centres of finance and production could now emerge in areas that were outside the direct control of the old industrial nations. Trade flowed not within national/imperial borders but across them. Both capital and labour began to move more freely across frontiers. Global capitalism may not have been new but it was certainly transformed and entered a phase of exceptional dynamism.

Global manufacturing

While the international division of labour prevailed, wage labour was mainly concentrated in the industrial societies. It certainly existed in the mines, the plantations, and the commercial agriculture of the Third World but in localized pockets, often in an intermediate or intermittent form, combined with other ways of making a living through peasant agriculture or trading activities. In this new era, capital's search for labour has, according to David Coates, during the last 30 years doubled the size of the 'world proletariat' to some 3 billion people.

The main vehicle of the spread of capitalist production has been the transnational corporation. There was a particularly fast growth of these corporations during the last quarter of the 20th century, with their numbers increasing from 7,000 in 1973 to 26,000 in 1993. Their investment in operations abroad rose particularly rapidly after 1985. Although much of this went into other industrial societies, investment in developing countries mounted sharply in the 1990s.

One of the best examples of this process is the growth of

10. **Cheap labour in the Mexico *maquiladora* plants**

manufacturing plants, known as *maquiladoras*, in Mexico. This began when in 1965 Mexico allowed factories within ten miles of its border with the United States to import raw materials and parts duty-free, if the finished product was re-exported. Their growth accelerated after the 1993 NAFTA Agreement removed the remaining barriers to trade. American, European, and eventually Japanese capital has moved in to exploit the cheap labour available in Mexico, and thousands of manufacturing and assembly plants, mainly in the vehicle, electronic, and textiles industries, have been set up along the border. Managers come in by car daily from their homes in the United States, while carless workers are bussed in from shanty towns.

Labour is cheap there not only because of its plentiful supply but also because it is unorganized and unregulated. Attempts to create independent trade unions have been crushed by the combined efforts of employers and government. The NAFTA Agreement contained rights for workers and protection for unions but these parts of it have not been implemented. American unions with an obvious interest in reducing the competition from cheap labour in Mexico have tried to organize Mexican workers and invoke the labour clauses of NAFTA but without much success. Health, safety, and environmental regulations are non-existent or very weakly enforced. The Mexican government has had a clear interest in turning a blind eye, since the *maquiladoras* make a major contribution to the Mexican economy by providing employment, around a million jobs at the beginning of this century, and making the second largest contribution, after oil, to foreign exchange earnings.

Asia has recently provided an even bigger attraction to capital, especially Japanese capital, which has moved in a series of waves into the countries of the Far East. Production in Japan became increasingly expensive as the rapid growth of Japanese industry after the Second World War led to shortages of land and labour, and prices rose at home. In the 1970s and 1980s Japanese capital moved in search of cheaper labour into the 'tiger economies' of Hong Kong, Taiwan, Singapore, and South Korea. As production became more expensive there, a second wave of capital moved from Japan and the 'tigers' into Indonesia, Malaysia, and Thailand. More recently a third wave of investment has gone into China and Vietnam. China seems to be currently *the* destination for capital and is threatening to lure away from Mexico the corporations that had earlier invested there.

The spread of manufacturing into these countries has particularly drawn young women into wage labour. They reportedly constitute some 60–70% of the *maquiladora* labour force in Mexico. The Nike and Gap factories in South-East Asia have been accused of employing girls under the age of 16, in spite of laws and guidelines prohibiting the exploitation of child labour. Capitalism combines with patriarchy to obtain the cheapest labour, for women are generally paid less than men, subject to male control, and

11. Cheap labour for Nike in Vietnam

disposable, since they can be returned to the household if the demand for labour drops.

This spread of wage labour has resulted in a global weakening of the power of labour. In the old industrial societies collective organization had enabled workers to reduce the power differential between capital and labour. Competition from cheap and unregulated labour abroad has undermined this collective power and unions have found it very difficult to extend labour organization to include overseas workers. As consumers, workers in the old industrial societies have certainly benefited, since cheaper labour abroad and greater international competition have lowered the prices of the goods that they buy, but real wages in the old industrial societies have, none the less, been in decline since the 1980s. Furthermore, as capital has become more mobile, nation-states have had to compete for it. Anti-union legislation of the kind enacted in 1980s Britain was justified in part by the argument that it made Britain attractive to the Japanese and Korean capital moving into the European Union during the 1980s and 1990s.

Global telework

It is not only manufacturing that has moved out of the old industrial societies, for most office work, such as typing, telephone-answering, data-processing, software development and problem-solving, can now be done at a distance. Advances in information and communication technology have made it particularly easy to transfer this kind of work to cheaper locations abroad, where wages and office costs are much lower. As with manufacturing and for the same reasons, it is commonly young women who are employed in this work.

Call-centres have been Britain's fastest growing source of employment, replacing the jobs lost in manufacturing, but now these jobs in turn are being moved overseas. Banks, insurance companies, travel agencies, telecom and rail companies, are transferring call-centre operations from Britain to China, India, and Malaysia. Similarly, French companies are moving jobs of this kind to Francophone countries in Africa. American companies have long since moved call-centre and data-processing work to the Caribbean.

It is a considerable advantage to be in an English-speaking part of the world, which has given some Caribbean islands and India a head start, though having English alone is not enough. Some training is, of course, needed and those working in telephone-answering services in India are trained in Western pronunciation and conversation. Effective call-centre operations also need careful management by 'relationship managers', who can strike a balance between efficiency considerations and customer service. Software development requires higher-level skills but India, especially the city of Bangalore, has become a major centre of software production, because of the availability of a highly educated, English-speaking workforce. Such high-profile companies as Texas Instruments, Motorola, Hewlett Packard, and IBM have set up software (and hardware) production there.

This is not only a matter of poor countries providing cheaper labour than rich countries but also of intense competition between the poor countries themselves. Barbados and Jamaica, where telework has long been established, have met a growing competition from other Caribbean islands and Central America. The Caribbean as a whole faces competition from the even cheaper labour available in India, the Philippines, Malaysia, and China. The ease with which telework operations can be set up means that there are few limits to the spread of its more routine and low-skilled forms.

Global tourism

International tourism is not often mentioned in accounts of the global spread of capitalism, but its growth is one of the most striking manifestations of the increasing economic connections between countries. Between 1950 and 2001 international tourist arrivals increased from 25 million a year to nearly 700 million. Tourism has become the main earner of foreign exchange in many of the world's poorest countries.

International tourism spreads capitalist practices into parts of the world that have been little touched historically by the growth of capitalism. It can penetrate into areas that have little capacity to produce goods or other services for the world market. Indeed, remote or undeveloped places, from Macchu Pichu on the eastern slopes of the Andes to Himalayan kingdoms, can be particularly attractive to tourists because they are remote or traditional. Tourism then creates employment in paid labour in bar and hotel work. It generates a greater demand for food production and transport, and may well provide the basis for the local manufacturing of souvenirs and faking of relics. The earnings from tourism can increase the circulation of money, lead to the import of manufactured goods, and establish new consumption patterns.

A process of commodification takes place as cultural practices, wildlife, sights, and views acquire a monetary value that they never had before. Customs may lose their authenticity when commercialized and nature may become less natural, though commercialization can at least enable their survival in a modified form. In an increasingly capitalist world, the only way of ensuring the survival of cultural practices and natural sights is to find ways of making profit out of them. Furthermore, the preservation principle can itself become the basis of an industry, as in the eco-tourism promoted by Costa Rica.

Global tourism has also been responsible for another process of commodification through sex tourism, as the bodies of both adults and children in poor countries have acquired a monetary value. The scale of sex tourism is huge. It was reported in 1999 that in the

United States alone more than 25 companies offered sex tours to Asian destinations. The Internet World Sex Guide provides information and reports on the availability, services, and prices of sex workers in every country in the world, with links to help people make their travel arrangements. The guide does not provide information about the availability of sex with children, but this is one of the main attractions of sex tourism since it enables adults to engage in this in distant and unregulated places, with apparently less risk than in their countries of origin.

Global tourism is clearly not an unmixed blessing, and even if it does bring some economic rewards to the societies receiving the tourists, one must bear in mind that much of the profit is expatriated by the foreign-owned corporations – airlines, hotel chains, and travel companies – that dominate this trade.

Global agriculture

In exploring these examples of global capitalism, we have rather neglected agriculture. Arguably, global agriculture is nothing new and has long flourished in the tea plantations of India and Sri Lanka or the fruit plantations of Central America. The international division of labour established in the 19th century created new markets in the industrial societies for the agricultural products of the rest of the world and Western corporations invested capital in their large-scale production.

In agriculture too, however, there has been growing international competition and capitalist production has spread. In the 1990s there was a crisis in the banana industry, which was producing more bananas than the market could absorb. American fruit corporations, notably Dole, began to shift production to Ecuador, where wages and other labour costs were substantially lower and there were no labour unions (at the same time existing unions came under attack in Central America). These corporations also

12. Large-scale banana production by Dole in Ecuador

used the World Trade Organization (WTO) to pressurize the European Union to end its preferential treatment of the banana growers in the ex-colonial territories of Africa and the Caribbean, where bananas were grown largely by small farmers with higher costs, who in a free market could not hope to compete successfully with the corporations. Eventually a compromise was reached that gave some protection to the small producers, while attempts have also been made to unionize the workers in Ecuador, but the fate of both the union and the small producers remains uncertain.

Small producers have also found themselves driven in other ways towards capitalist agriculture. Vandana Shiva has argued that agriculture is becoming increasingly dominated by highly concentrated 'life science corporations', which cut across agribusiness, biotechnology, and the chemical and pharmaceutical industries. These corporations sell genetically engineered seed, which can produce large crops and, it is claimed, cure deficiency diseases, through, for example, adding vitamin A to rice. This kind of agriculture can be very productive of cash crops but it requires the extensive use of the pesticides and herbicides also sold by these corporations, and large amounts of water. The environmental consequences are disastrous, as scarce water resources are used up, chemical pollution increases, and biodiversity is lost. Farmers not only become dependent on the corporations but also go into debt, since considerable investment is required, and can then end up losing their land if poor harvests or other disasters destroy their capacity to service their debts. Small-scale agriculture loses its viability and large capital-intensive units take over.

Allied to this process is a commodification of nature, as plants, seeds, genes, and water, which were previously natural resources, often available freely to all, become commodities that have a monetary value. Knowledge itself has become commodified. The WTO's Trade Related Intellectual Property Rights Agreement requires countries to allow the patenting of information about plant strains and genetic material. Vandana Shiva argues that this means:

> The knowledge of the poor is being converted into the property of global corporations, creating a situation where the poor will have to pay for the seeds and medicines they have evolved and have used to meet their own needs for nutrition and health care.

Global money

The spread of the capitalist practices that we have been examining inevitably generated an increasing circulation of money, but the truly astonishing rise in its international circulation during the last quarter of the 20th century was mainly the result of speculative money movements. By the end of the century trading in foreign currencies amounted to US \$1.5 trillion *a day*, a sum equivalent to more than the *annual* Gross National Product of the UK. International investment, most of which was speculative, increased by a factor of nearly 200 between 1970 and 1997, according to Manuel Castells.

As Castells has emphasized, technological advances made possible this vast expansion of international currency dealing and investment. This was partly a matter of communications, for geo-stationary satellites, the digital transmission of data, and computer networks increased not only the speed of transactions but also the sheer amount of business that could be handled. It was also a matter of financial technology and innovation; many new ways of investing in the markets and channelling the capital of both companies and individuals into them were created by a flourishing financial services industry. It was new financial instruments and products as well as new communications equipment that generated the flow of money across borders.

The now infamous 'derivatives', of the kind traded so disastrously by Nick Leeson (see Chapter 1), were in the 1980s and 1990s the most sophisticated new financial instruments. Money was also more straightforwardly channelled through investment funds into the 'emerging markets' that began to attract investment in the 1980s. There were opportunities here for investors to buy cheaply into newly industrializing countries and then realize gains when prices rose. The financial industries of the affluent societies rapidly created a whole range of such funds to tap into the savings of ordinary people. The Asian economic crisis of the later 1990s (see Chapter 6) then rapidly destroyed much of the value accumulated in these funds.

It was not just technology and financial innovation that accounted for these flows of money across borders. The floating of currencies in the 1970s created new uncertainties and new opportunities, which stimulated currency trading and futures markets. 'Floating' meant that currency values were determined not by official rates but by the market, rising and falling according to the supply of a currency and the demand for it. There was greater uncertainty for companies that needed foreign currencies for their operations and they therefore needed to protect themselves by trading in futures. Above all, however, currency trading increased because of the greater opportunities that floating rates provided for speculation.

It is of some interest to consider briefly why currencies floated in this way. Previously, under the system set up at the Bretton Woods conference of 1944, currency values had been fixed in relation to the dollar, which in turn had its value fixed in relation to gold. The stability this provided enabled the expansion of international trade and a period of steady economic growth. In the early 1970s, however, it proved increasingly difficult to maintain the fixed value of the dollar and the United States government was forced to devalue it. There were particular reasons for the devaluation of the dollar at this time, notably the consequences of American government spending on the Vietnam War, but the Bretton Woods system had anyway come under a growing strain.

This was because fixed official exchange rates could only be maintained if governments either pursued unpopular policies or controlled the movement of money across their borders. If a growing trade deficit put pressure on the existing rate, and speculators began to bet on a devaluation, governments could take harsh economic measures to maintain the value of their currency. They could, for example, reduce consumption in order to curb imports. This was, however, politically very difficult in democratic societies. Alternatively, they could stop speculators moving money around, and this they tried to do through exchange controls. But it became harder to control money movements, as trade increased, as holdings of some countries' currencies, above all the US dollar, accumulated abroad, and as larger amounts of money began to move between countries.

The deregulatory spirit of the remarketized capitalism of the 1980s, which we examined in Chapter 3, also played its part in all this. Exchange rates fixed by the state and controls on the international movement of money did not accord with the renewed belief in free markets and competition. Greater competition between financial centres provided much of the momentum behind the deregulation of financial markets and financial innovation. Financial industries linked with stock markets were growing in economic importance and the health of these industries depended on their capacity to draw the international flow of money through their markets. Competition between the established financial centres of the world lay behind the City of London's 'big bang' deregulation in October 1987, as London tried to catch up with New York. But competition was also coming from new financial centres, and by the 1990s there were some 35 stock markets in developing countries. Some have become highly sophisticated financial centres, and it was through dealing on the Simex financial futures exchange in Singapore that Nick Leeson made and lost his reputation.

How global is global?

Capitalist institutions and practices have been spreading across the world, but at this point we must halt a moment and consider quite how global 'global capitalism' really is.

The circulation of money across the world has increased but is this 'financial globalization'? Even though new financial centres have emerged in developing countries and investment in 'emerging markets' became, for a time at least, fashionable, most of the money still flows between North America, Europe, and Japan. Castells has pointed out that in 1998 the emerging markets accounted for only 7% of the world's capital, even though their countries contained around 85% of the world's population. Furthermore, the money flowing into emerging markets at least temporarily diminished after the 1997–8 financial crises in Asia and Russia alarmed foreign investors. During the years 1998–2001 only $19 billion flowed into the emerging markets, as compared with $655 billion during 1994–7.

The same argument applies to global tourism. Much of the international circulation of tourists is between the already developed countries of Europe, North America, and Japan. In 2001 the world's top four earners from international tourism were the United States, Spain, France, and Italy, though significantly China came fifth.

Capitalist production has spread, and much more investment went into poor countries in the 1990s than the 1980s, but it was still heavily concentrated in a small number of countries, notably China, Brazil, and Mexico, with very little finding its way into Africa. According to OECD figures, roughly one-third of the foreign direct investment received by developing countries in the 1990s went to China. In the year 2000, the whole of Africa (excluding South Africa) received less than 1% of total world foreign direct investment, a sum equivalent to the amount received by one European country with a population of only 5 million – Finland.

While it is often claimed that global capitalism is integrating the world, international differences are actually increasing. Some previously poor countries, such as the Asian tiger economies, have hauled themselves up by their bootstraps and partially closed the gap between themselves and the rich countries. They are, however, the exceptions and, as the United Nations Human Development Reports have clearly shown, the gap between the richest and poorest countries has hugely increased. In 1820 the five richest countries in the world were three times as rich as the five poorest. By 1950, they were 35 times as rich; by 1970, 44 times; and by 1992, 72 times. The world has become steadily more *divided* by international differences in wealth.

One of the problems with the term 'globalization' is the implication that a new level of global organization has emerged that transcends national units, as with the term 'global corporation'. There are certainly many transnational corporations, in the sense that corporations operate in different countries and across national boundaries, but most operate in only a few countries and are hardly global in character. They are often seen as flouting the nation-state, transferring employment abroad, and often avoiding the payment of taxes in their home country, but all are based in a nation-state somewhere and most actually have the bulk of their assets and provide most of their employment in this state. They exploit the facilities of their home nation-state, its infrastructure and institutions, and use its power to promote and assist their operations abroad. They may provide employment in poor countries, but they also exploit their cheap labour, drive out local competitors, and channel profits back to their home state. As Peter Dicken has argued, transnational corporations are also national corporations, and most cannot really be described as global at all.

The notion of 'global capitalism' must then be used with caution. The flow of money and investment is so unevenly spread across the globe that it is more than a little misleading to describe it as 'global', while commonly used global terms, such as 'global capitalism', 'global economy', and 'global society' gloss over widening international differences and the continuing importance of national units and national governments.

Global capitalist dominance

In one respect there can, however, be little doubt that capitalism has gone global and that is in the elimination of alternative systems.

The year 1989 saw the main global alternative, state socialism, begin to collapse. Gorbachev initiated a regime of 'restructuring and openness' in the Soviet Union, which also began to loosen its grip on its East European satellites. The Soviet economy had operated on the basis of central planning and the bureaucratic direction of the economy, with markets operating only at the margins. It has been castigated and ridiculed for its inefficiency, its low productivity, its poor overall economic performance, and pollution of the environment, which all apparently made it living proof of the superiority of capitalism. Its record of industrialization and substantial economic growth, its maintenance of full employment and low inflation, and its capable provision of education and health care have now been largely forgotten, though no doubt many Russians still remember the stability and security it once provided.

It collapsed largely because it could not compete with the more dynamic capitalist economies of the West. Expectations had been rising in Russia and Eastern Europe, for in a world of growing communication, people could not be insulated from the individualist consumer culture of the West. Economies operating under the constraints of state socialism could not meet these expectations, or at least not while so much of their resources were devoted to military production. It was arguably the burden imposed by the Cold War that was insupportable, and Reagan's 'Star Wars' programme may well have been the final blow, since it sharply escalated the military-industrial competition between the superpowers.

Gorbachev had tried to introduce a programme of gradual reform, but no gradual transition from a command to a market economy occurred. Once state direction ceased, economic paralysis followed, and under Yeltsin's leadership an attempt was made to jolt Russia into capitalism. The 'shock therapy' administered to the economy in 1991 freed prices from state control and by the end of 1994 had privatized three-quarters of Russia's medium and large enterprises. The consequences were catastrophic for most ordinary people. According to John Gray's account, between 1991 and 1996 consumer prices increased by a factor of 1,700 and some 45 million people fell into poverty. The policy of shock therapy was halted and, under the leadership of Putin, Russia may well now be moving back towards a more state-controlled form of capitalism. This would not, however, be a return to state socialism, for its structures have been discredited and dismantled, while some influential groups now have vested interests in capitalism, and Russia has become integrated into the world capitalist economy.

While the collapse of state socialism removed the main alternative model, developing societies were forced by financial pressures and international institutions to conform to the dominant American model of capitalism. A key role in this was played by American-dominated international financial institutions – the World Bank and the International Monetary Fund (IMF). Both were created during the Second World War by the same Bretton Woods conference that set up the postwar system of fixed exchange rates. The World Bank was to assist countries with postwar reconstruction and development, while the IMF was charged with maintaining international economic stability. Although their functions were different, in the 1980s these institutions began to jointly promote the free-market ideologies and policies that increasingly held sway in the United States and other leading industrial societies. Like other international institutions, they were dominated by their most powerful members.

They advocated three key and inter-related policies. The first of these was fiscal austerity to reduce wasteful government spending and eliminate loose monetary policies leading to inflation. The second was privatization to get rid of inefficient public enterprises, introduce market discipline, and also reduce government spending. The third was liberalization, the removal of barriers to trade, with the assistance of the WTO, founded in 1995, and the ending of government interference with the operation of markets. These policies were implemented through 'conditionality', that is loans were conditional on the pursuit of such policies. The high dependence of developing societies on loans meant that they were in a very weak position to resist such policies, however inappropriate they might be. Indeed, these policies were implemented in developing countries more rigorously than they were in the developed societies themselves. The United States, Europe, and Japan have all heavily protected and subsidized their agriculture.

Joseph Stiglitz, a senior figure at the World Bank between 1997 and 2000, has written a scathing critique of these policies, particularly as implemented by the IMF. He was not opposed to the policies themselves, which could bring benefits in some circumstances, but to their indiscriminate and over-hasty imposition. In inappropriate situations austerity could destroy valuable projects dependent on government expenditure and create mass unemployment, while privatization could lead to the plundering of public assets and higher prices for consumers. As for liberalization, particularly of financial markets, this could simply open the door to an invasion by foreign capital. Indeed, Stiglitz suggests that the IMF's policies in this regard were often driven by its links with Wall Street financial interests.

The policies were implemented as though there were no alternatives. Stiglitz draws a contrast between the experience of Russia and the experience of China. IMF advice led Russia into 'shock therapy' and the creation of mass poverty, while China's opposite strategy of gradualist transition 'entailed the largest reduction in poverty in history in such a short time span'. The secret of China's success was that instead of destroying old institutions in the expectation that new ones would then naturally emerge, China allowed new capitalist enterprises to develop within the existing social order. It did not make the mistake of mass privatization but rather created the conditions within which a private sector could emerge and flourish, following, as it happens, the advice given by Stiglitz!

This was not, of course, just a matter of choosing the right policies and policy advisers, for China's more effective elite, with a stronger economy and state, were in a much better position than the paralysed rulers of a disintegrating Soviet Union to go their own way towards capitalism and control the transition. Shocks and conflicts may, anyway, lie ahead for the Chinese model, which appears to be making a successful economic transition from communism to capitalism, but is also creating a dislocated proletariat with few channels for the expression of discontent in the absence of a political transition.

The state socialist alternative has collapsed and, as the only viable economic system, capitalism has become globally dominant. There can be no doubt that capitalism has delivered goods and services in much greater quantities and with far greater choice than state socialism ever did. This does not, however, mean that there is only one route to economic success, for there are different routes to capitalism and, as we saw in the last chapter, different ways of organizing it. We should not confuse the elimination of alternatives *to* capitalism with the elimination of alternatives *within* it.

The myths of global capitalism

'Global capitalism' is a short-hand phrase that conveys the idea that in recent years the institutions and practices of capitalism have spread into new areas of the world and connected distant parts closely together in new ways. There can be no doubt that this has happened and that there has consequently been a profound transformation of the world in which we live. Capitalism is the globally dominant system and will continue to be so in the foreseeable future.

In the course of this chapter, we have, however, found that the notion of global capitalism has also generated powerful and misleading myths. *Myth one* is that global capitalism is recent, for it has deep historical roots. *Myth two* is that capital circulates globally, when in reality most of it moves between a small group of rich countries. *Myth three* is that capitalism is now organized globally rather than nationally, for international differences are as important as ever and nation-states continue to play a key role in the activities of transnational corporations. *Myth four* is that global capitalism integrates the world, since the more global capitalism has become, the more divided the world has become by international inequalities of wealth.

Chapter 6
Crisis? What crisis?

Those living in the midst of an economic crisis may well feel that their world is collapsing. They may indeed think that the whole capitalist system is coming to an end. Crises of capitalism are not, however, exceptional events but rather a normal part of the functioning of a capitalist society. In the 19th century they became a regular feature of economic life, though crisis mechanisms that are familiar in today's world actually appeared centuries earlier. This chapter begins with the 'tulipomania' of 17th-century Holland, which shows the same basic mechanisms in operation as the recent dotcom and information technology bubbles.

The tulip bubble in 17th-century Amsterdam

After their 16th-century arrival from Turkey, tulips, especially the more exotic and rarer specimens, had become highly prized in 17th-century Holland. Tulip growing spread in the rich alluvial soil of Holland but scarce supply and high demand resulted in rapidly rising prices. Its high profitability attracted many into this trade, where little investment was required and money could easily be made.

The high demand for bulbs led to rapid changes in the bulb trade. At first bulbs were sold in large quantities, sometimes in complete beds, but as demand grew these were broken down into smaller units until individual bulbs, particularly those of the most valuable varieties, were traded. Then a market developed in the outgrowths from the bulb, the clones from which future bulbs could be grown. Finally, in the 1630s, the tulip trade generated the market in tulip futures that led to the 'tulipomania' of 1636-7.

How did this happen? Initially, the trading season was short and lasted only a few months after the flowering and lifting of the bulbs. To meet expanding demand traders began buying and selling tulips that were still in the ground. They were now in effect buying and selling bulb futures. Promissory notes specified the details of the tulip bought and when it would be lifted, while a sign in the ground identified the owner. It was then but a small step to trade in the notes rather than the bulbs, for rapidly rising bulb prices gave the notes themselves an increasing value.

The tulip futures trade became a wildly speculative bubble, where prices were pushed up not by the demand for bulbs but the demand for the 'paper' futures. Since only a deposit had to be made on the future purchase, a small amount of money went a long way, so long as the contract note could be unloaded on someone else at a profit before full payment became due. As contract dates approached, dealing became increasingly frenzied and the notes circulated faster. Prices eventually rose to the point at which no-one was prepared to buy and then suddenly collapsed. There was no real demand for many of the quite ordinary tulips that had been drawn into the speculative dealing at the height of the boom. Since no-one actually wanted these bulbs, the right to buy them in the future was ultimately worthless and there was, therefore, no floor to the crashing market.

Trading in futures was the central mechanism in the inflation of this bubble and at this time was already an established practice of merchant capitalism but it was, interestingly, not the merchants who were the main players. Some did become involved but the really big merchants, who were busy making relatively risk-free money from their monopolies, seem to have held aloof. The bubble was inflated as ordinary people, such as weavers, bricklayers, carpenters, and cobblers, became involved. They raised capital by using up their savings, borrowing, mortgaging their property, or making payments in kind. Simon Schama gives the example of the purchase of just one rare bulb with 'two *last* of wheat and four of rye, four fat oxen, eight pigs, a dozen sheep, two oxheads of wine, four tons of butter, a thousand pounds of cheese, a bed, some clothing and a silver beaker'.

The trading of bulbs and notes was not carried out in the Amsterdam stock exchange, though there was plenty of other speculative activity going on there, but in the taverns where 'colleges' of traders met and drank. These colleges developed their own secret procedures, trading rituals, and festivities, a poor man's version of those at the stock exchange. Speculative capitalism was then, as it is now, not just the province of sophisticated financiers but also a popular activity.

Crises of the 19th century

Serious as its consequences were for those involved, the bursting of the tulip bubble did not impact significantly on the economy as a whole. There was not at this time a sufficiently high integration of economic activities to spread a crisis in one area to the whole economy. It was the growth of capitalist production that produced the necessary linkages to make crises economy-wide. Furthermore, capitalist production actually generated new crisis mechanisms, which Karl Marx analysed.

Marx argued that capitalism was prone to crises because production was separated from consumption. In pre-capitalist societies they were closely related, since most production was for more or less immediate consumption. Under capitalism, goods were increasingly produced for sale in markets and this relationship became more distant. Goods were produced in the expectation that they could be sold, but the market might be unable to absorb them. Marx described capitalism as anarchic because production was no longer directly regulated by the needs of those consuming its products.

A tendency to overproduce was in fact built into capitalist production. Competition between producers generated a pressure to expand production, since higher volume reduced costs, cheapened prices, and enlarged market share. When the amount of goods produced exceeded the demand for them, there would be an overproduction crisis and prices would fall, eventually below the level at which profits could be made. This not only damaged the industry concerned but had knock-on effects that spread the crisis. Investment would decline and hit those industries producing machinery. Workers would be laid off or wages lowered, which would further reduce consumer demand. In these ways, overproduction generated vicious circles, leading to closures and bankruptcies, and high levels of unemployment. Mass unemployment then resulted in a social crisis, for in a capitalist economy people were in a quite new way dependent on wage labour for their survival. Such crises occurred roughly every ten years during the first half of the 19th century.

Although unemployment caused great suffering and some capitalists went out of business, these crises did not destroy capitalism. Indeed, Marx argued that it was crises that made it possible for capitalism to continue, since they eliminated the strains of overproduction, forced out the least efficient producers, and enabled the renewed operation of virtuous circles, once closures and bankruptcies had reduced production to a level closer to demand. Similarly, lower wages increased profitability and cheaper prices stimulated demand. Lower interest rates made it cheaper to borrow money for investment. Production could start to expand again, employment would rise, and there would be more people with money in their pockets to buy goods.

Capitalism would therefore expand its way out of crisis but, he argued in the *Communist Manifesto*, this expansion would only lead to 'more extensive and more destructive crises'. This did not mean, as some of his followers have thought, that Marx believed that capitalism would end in some huge economic collapse. It would come to an end only when overthrown by the workers it exploited. Certain tendencies in its development would facilitate this eventual overthrow. The advance of technology and the concentration of ownership would increase the size of units of production and workers would be concentrated in larger masses that would be easier to organize. Crises would certainly play a part in all this by radicalizing workers through their experience of them. They would also be radicalized by the widening gulf between the wealth of the increasingly small group of capitalists who enjoyed the profits of capital and the poverty of the frequently unemployed masses.

Ownership did become more concentrated, units of production increased in size, and workers became more organized, but Marx's expectation that the working class would become increasingly radical and ultimately revolutionary has not been borne out. Workers were coerced into an acceptance of capitalism by their economic dependence on employment and the repression of revolutionary movements that sought to overthrow the capitalist system. They have also been incorporated through their organizations into the political structures of capitalist societies, and seduced by the flood of goods and services that capitalist production has provided. There was, anyway, no crisis of a sufficient scale to threaten the capitalist economic system until the 1930s.

The Great Depression in the 1930s

A period of reasonably steady, if not crisis-free, growth lasted from the middle of the 19th century until the First World War and this apparently resumed in the 1920s. The ending of the First World War had, however, left the world economy in a fragile state. The City of London's stabilizing financial dominance had now passed into history and international economic relationships were disorganized and unstable during the 1920s. Furthermore, the war and its aftermath had left many countries, above all Germany, heavily in debt and with weakened economies that made it difficult to service and repay debts. This was the background to the Great Depression of the 1930s, a depression so deep and extensive that Eric Hobsbawm considers it 'amounted to something very close to the collapse of the capitalist world economy'.

There had been many signs in the 1920s that all was not well with the world economy, but it was the 1929 collapse of the Wall Street stock market in New York that signalled the plunge into depression. New York prices crashed in October 1929 but then continued downwards until they hit bottom in June 1932, having lost over 80% of their value since their September 1929 peak.

Cumulative mechanisms depressed the economy. Production declined throughout the industrial world and this resulted in sharply rising unemployment, which reduced demand and led to the further contraction of production. In the United States, industrial production fell by one-third during the years 1929–31 and over a quarter of the labour force was unemployed at the bottom of the slump. Unemployed workers could no longer pay the interest on their house loans and this threatened the solvency of local banks. They could no longer afford to buy consumer goods, especially cars, and American car production halved, throwing more people out of work. Low state benefits at this time not only made unemployment a far worse experience than it is in today's industrial societies, they also meant that mass unemployment could eliminate the purchasing power of a large part of the population.

This was not just a crisis of the industrial world, for there was also a severe depression in agriculture. As consumer demand declined and stocks accumulated, the prices of agricultural products fell, tea

13. Traders watch the ticker tape as Wall Street crashes in 1929

and wheat prices dropping by two-thirds and the price of silk by
three-quarters. Farmers reacted by increasing production in a vain
attempt to maintain their incomes but this led to prices falling even
further. The dominant images of the 1930s are of the unemployed
in Europe and America lining up at soup kitchens or setting off on
hunger marches. Countries such as Argentina, Brazil, and Cuba, or
Australia and New Zealand, with economies dependent on their

14. Labour is auctioned to the highest bidder during the 1930s Depression in the United States

export of food and raw materials to the industrial societies, were equally devastated.

The 1930s demonstrated the capitalist world economy's *vulnerability* to crisis. The problem was not so much the occurrence of crisis, for, as we have seen, crises are part of the normal machinery of capitalism, but the ensuing crash of capitalist economies across the world, as cumulative mechanisms spread and deepened the crisis. Three main sources of this vulnerability can be identified.

There was first the huge growth in productive capacity that had taken place over the previous century. This meant that equally huge levels of demand were necessary if production was to be absorbed and applied not only to the production of manufactured goods but also to the production of food and other primary products. Insufficient demand for products has been interpreted not only as overproduction but also as underconsumption by poorly paid workers. Either way, the increasing scale of production and the growing numbers of people employed in it meant that a failure of consumption to keep pace with production could precipitate a rapid downward spiral of the economy, as workers, who were also consumers, lost their jobs.

The second was the international division of labour that integrated the world economy. The industrial societies produced the manufactured goods and the rest of the world concentrated on producing food and raw materials. If demand fell in the industrial societies, the primary producers exporting, say, beef, coffee, or sugar, to them found that their sales, prices, and incomes dropped. When their incomes dropped, the overseas markets for industrial goods declined. Some historians consider the depression began in the primary producer countries and was then transmitted to the industrial societies, while others have argued the opposite, but, either way, a crisis in one group of countries was inevitably transmitted to the other and then reverberated between them. Global economic integration was another mechanism that amplified the depression.

The third was the tension between international trade and national protection. As the first industrial nation, Britain had promoted free-trade policies, which maximized the markets for its products. When other countries industrialized, they were inevitably more protectionist, since their infant industries needed protection in order to establish themselves. A growing international competition then generated ever more calls for national protection. British economic dominance and global economic growth had none the less maintained free trade until the First World War, but after this war, and partly because of it, the international economy was no longer dominated by Britain and no longer characterized by stable economic growth.

When domestic production faced a crisis, it was hard to resist the temptation to protect the national economy against foreign competition and as soon as action of this kind was taken by one country, others followed. In particular, the introduction of extensive tariff protection of its economy by the United States in 1930 triggered a retaliation by other countries. Furthermore, the 19th-century division of the world between competing empires provided the industrial societies both with an illusion of self-sufficiency and ready-made structures within which they could shelter. The result was a cumulative decline of world trade that made the depression worse.

Out of the depression emerged a new set of policies designed to prevent it ever happening again. Governments were accustomed to respond to depression by cutting their expenditure or raising taxes, in order to balance their books when declining economic activity reduced their tax revenue. John Maynard Keynes argued that governments could counteract tendencies towards depression by injecting demand into the economy, by borrowing and spending or by lowering taxes. These 'Keynesian' policies began to make an impact in some countries in the later 1930s, though it was above all the huge state expenditure generated by the Second World War that hauled the global economy out of the depression.

From postwar boom to new crisis

During the quarter-century after the end of the Second World War it really did seem as though the crisis tendencies of capitalism had at last been mastered. Fears of a postwar return to high unemployment proved groundless. Governments thought they now knew how to use Keynesian policies to prevent crises getting out of control, though the steady economic growth of this period probably had little to do with their economic skills, for governments frequently mistimed their interventions and were as likely to reinforce as counteract the economic cycle. There were other underlying factors that fuelled the boom.

The heavy spending of the war period had not in fact stopped, for the United States was now engaged in a new war, the Cold War with the Soviet Union. This led not only to military expenditure overseas but also to the deliberate revival of the Japanese and European economies, since these areas were in the front line of the Cold War. It also led to the space race, as the United States reacted to Soviet success in putting Gagarin into space by pouring money into its own space programme. This was an expansive dynamism that was very different from the isolationist protectionism of the interwar period. The largest economy in the world was spreading economic growth across it.

Technological advance greatly increased production but an overproduction crisis was avoided because consumer demand too was steadily increasing. Higher productivity meant that the prices of goods came down, so that they fell increasingly within the reach of the workers who made them. Car ownership, for example, was spreading down the social scale. Greater productivity also allowed workers' wages to rise, while full employment maximized worker bargaining power.

Much of this growth was, however, at others' expense. The affluence of the industrial societies depended on the low prices of the primary products from the rest of the world. The low price of oil was particularly crucial, because it was not only a fuel but also the basis of a wide range of synthetic materials. These were substituted for the 'natural' products of the Third World and further drove down the prices they could command. Thus, new synthetic textiles diminished the demand for cotton. The relationship between the prices of manufactured goods and primary products changed to the disadvantage of the primary producers, who found that by 1970 manufactured goods were costing them one-third more than they had done in 1951.

In the 1970s all this changed, for the virtuous circles that had enabled the growth of the two previous decades turned vicious as the international economy hit the buffers. The clearest example of this was a rise in the prices of many primary products, notably oil, which steadily increased industrial costs and shop prices, both hitting profits and diminishing real wages and, therefore, reducing spending power. Profits were squeezed by wage increases, partly because of the continued growth of union organization and rivalries between unions, partly because workers reacted to price and tax increases by demanding wage increases that would maintain their standard of living. Another problem was that American military expenditure and imports had flooded the world with dollars that could no longer be absorbed by the existing international financial system based on fixed exchange rates.

The result was a crisis quite different in character to that of the 1930s. In the 1930s demand had collapsed but now there was too much demand, which forced prices and wages up. Furthermore, the floating of currencies after the collapse of fixed exchange rates relaxed monetary controls on inflation, for governments were now under less pressure to guard the value of their currency in order to maintain these rates.

Increasing international competition intensified the crisis. The recovery of Germany and Japan from the destruction wrought on their economies by defeat in the Second World War brought modern and highly efficient industries into production. This further increased the pressure on world resources and also generated a new overproduction crisis. Higher wages and raw material prices due to greater demand, followed by an overproduction that reduced the prices that companies could charge for their goods, made it much more difficult to make profits.

The impact of Japan on the profitability of the industries of the old industrial societies was particularly devastating, because in Japan government and industry cooperated very effectively in pursuing long-term policies designed to create new industries and capture markets, while Japanese productivity was much higher. It was the old industrial societies that faced particular problems in dealing with this crisis. Their development of managed capitalism had, as we saw in Chapter 3, restricted or replaced the market mechanisms that would have promoted a rapid rationalizing response. An effective response had to wait upon the remarketizing of their economies by the governments of the 1980s.

Instability

After the 1970s a new world of slower growth, greater instability, and frequent crises emerged. Growth rates in the last quarter of the 20th century were half those of the previous quarter. They also diverged sharply, with some countries, notably Australia, Ireland, and the Netherlands, growing much faster during the 1990s than the 1980s, while in a much larger group of countries, such as Germany, Italy, Japan, Korea, and Switzerland, growth rates fell back. Many countries were on the edge of crisis much of the time, but even strong national economies ran into trouble when growth bubbles burst. Crises could also spread easily from one country to another, as in the crisis of 1997–8, which began in the apparently strong economies of East Asia but then spread to Russia and later Brazil.

This was a world of intensified international competition. As we saw above, the growth of international competition was one of the processes that led to lower profitability in the old industrial societies during the 1970s. Lower profitability then resulted in companies seeking to restore profits by finding cheaper labour elsewhere. As industrial employment, whether in manufacturing or services, spread to new areas of the world, international competition increased even further. The collapse of the last great empire, that of the Soviet Union, allowed the countries of Eastern Europe to bring their considerable supplies of cheap labour into the capitalist world. The entry of China at least began to bring almost a quarter of the world's population into the capitalist world economy.

Higher production, resulting from increased capacity and also, of course, technological change, could be absorbed if demand increased as well, but global demand did not expand at the same rate as the supply of goods. After all, one reason why new centres of production emerged was the availability of cheap labour, and low wages did not generate much consumer demand. The lending of recycled oil money to Third World countries initially stimulated consumption there, but higher interest rates then left these countries with huge long-term debts, which a large part of their national incomes was devoted to servicing and paying off. As we saw in Chapter 5, international inequality steadily increased, which meant that consumption was more and more concentrated in the established industrial societies of America, Europe, and, by now, the Far East.

Consumer demand in these countries too was, however, faltering. Companies reduced wage costs in order to at least try to compete with cheap imports from the new industrializers, and real wages and therefore purchasing power declined. Privatization exposed cushioned state employees to the rigours of the open labour market. Labour was shifted from 'good jobs' in manufacturing to poorly paid service work. Higher unemployment in many countries further depressed consumer demand. Governments have been less willing to spend and more concerned to balance their budgets, in line with post-Keynesian economic orthodoxy. Global consumption has not therefore kept pace with global production, and overproduction has been an ever-present threat to profits, wages, and employment.

While one response to the declining profitability of production was to search for cheaper labour abroad, another was, as Arrighi has argued, to shift capital from investment in production to speculation in shares, currencies, and derivatives. As we saw in Chapter 5, huge amounts of money began to flow across national borders and became a new source of instability in the capitalist world economy, leading to the East Asian crisis of 1997.

Large amounts of money seeking investment in 'emerging markets' had moved into the apparently strong East Asian economies, but in 1997 fears about the stability of the Thai economy triggered a withdrawal of funds. This in turn led to the collapse of share prices and the currency, and bank failures. A similar sequence of events followed in Malaysia, Indonesia, Hong Kong, and South Korea. It did not stop there and crises followed in Russia and Brazil, as investors pulled money out of any economy judged to be weak. The ensuing recession in the immediately affected countries not only devastated their economies but impacted globally, as East Asian demand declined, hitting, for example, American agricultural and aircraft exports to the region.

This crisis demonstrated the new instability of the capitalist world economy in two ways. The fears that led to the withdrawal of funds from Thailand resulted at least in part from the threat to profits from increasing competition in the region as the producers of goods as various as microchips, steel, and cars multiplied. The crisis was then amplified by international financial integration and the ease with which money could now be moved into and out of national economies. Overproduction, increasing international competition, and the mobility of money interacted with each other to produce a crisis that bounced from one country to another for well over a year.

The information technology boom

A revolution in information and communication technology (ICT) seemed to provide an escape from this instability into a new era of economic growth. This was not only because of investment in 'silicon valleys' and the creation of new hardware and software products but also because these could enhance the productivity of many existing industries. According to the OECD, 'ICT is transforming economic activity, as the steam engine, railways and electricity have done in the past'. There can be little doubt that it has transformed people's work lives, through word-processing and computer-controlled production, geo-stationary satellites and mobile phones, the Internet and the Web, e-commerce and telework. According to the OECD, investment in ICT certainly contributed to economic growth during the 1990s, above all in the United States but in many other countries too, especially Australia and Finland.

There was, however, no escape from the cycle of boom and bust that has occurred so often in the history of capitalism, as e-commerce showed. *Lastminute.com* provides a good example. Founded in 1998, *Lastminute.com* was based on the idea that the Internet could be used to match companies desperate to unload unsold holidays or meals or hotel rooms on consumers looking for last-minute bargains. In March 2000, at the height of the dotcom boom, it was floated on the stock market at a price of £3.80p, which valued it higher than many well-established and profitable companies. Its price rose quickly to over £5 a share and its founders had apparently joined the ranks of the dotcom millionaires, but within a week the dotcom bubble had begun to deflate and *Lastminute*'s share price started to fall, dropping to 17p by September 2001. Although, as originally conceived, it had failed, *Lastminute* did survive, by turning itself into an Internet travel agency and using the capital it had raised through its flotation to buy up other companies. It was expected to make a small profit for the first time in the financial year 2002–3.

Lastminute was untypical in that it survived but typical in many other ways of the dotcom boom. Its initial funding came from venture capital and at first it struggled to raise the money it needed to stay in business but, after massive media publicity, banks competed for the right to float it on the stock market. At the time of its flotation (by Morgan Stanley) it was oversubscribed 47 times, even though it was expected to make a loss of £20 million that year. Its share price was not based on expected earnings but on the gains that could be made from rising prices in a stock-market boom. The frenzied competition for both its business and its shares was driven by the fear of missing out and fuelled by a media-hyped new

15. Martha Jane Fox and Brent Hoberman, the founders of *Lastminute.com*, looking pleased with themselves just before the company was floated in March 2000

technology euphoria. As with all bubbles, some investors eventually decided that the peak had been reached and started to cash in their gains. Once the normal criteria of profitability were reasserted, the non-existence of profits in the foreseeable future meant that prices fell towards zero.

The telecommunications industry experienced a similar rise, if not quite such a catastrophic fall. In Britain, privatization had removed public-sector restraints and BT embarked on a buying spree aimed at turning it into a global corporation. BT bought companies in other countries, attempted to merge with major American corporations, and competed for mobile phone licences. This last proved ruinous for all involved, as governments auctioned these licences to the highest bidder, raising £22.5 billion in Britain and £31 billion in Germany, though those paying for the licences could only guess at how much they might earn from them. The outcome was hugely indebted telecom companies. BT's debts peaked at £28 billion and to reduce them to a supportable level it had to sell off at a heavy loss the overseas companies it had bought and its mobile phone operation.

One of BT's major competitors was WorldCom, the second largest long-distance phone company in the United States and its biggest Internet carrier. WorldCom was worth $180 billion at its peak and employed 80,000 people, but in July 2002 it filed for bankruptcy, after disclosing that it had misleadingly inflated its profits by some $9 billion. As this came hard on the heels of the similar Enron scandal, there was great press interest in the corporation's fraudulent accounting practices, but these concealed other problems. Starting as a small Mississippi phone company, WorldCom had acquired 60 companies in 15 years until its expansion was halted in 2000 by European and American regulators, who feared that a proposed merger (with Sprint) would give it a global stranglehold on Internet traffic. WorldCom had in fact already bought more capacity in broadband than the existing demand justified, while it also met growing competition from new entrants to the long-distance phone market and mobile phone companies. This was another story of over-expansion, increasing competition, excess capacity, indebtedness, insufficient earnings, and unprofitability.

The ICT revolution had stimulated a burst of economic growth in some countries and conferred many benefits on at least some of the people who lived in them, but it had not solved the problems of the capitalist world economy. The ICT sector went through the same cycle of expansion, overproduction, increasing competition, and contraction that earlier industries transformed by technological advances had experienced. ICT had also made its own unique contribution to the instability of capitalism by enabling the faster movement of larger quantities of money across the world.

A deflating world?

Some economic commentators now fear that the world economy is entering a deflationary period of falling prices. If prices fall, and the prices of goods at least have been falling, this encourages people to hold back on spending, since goods will become even cheaper in the future. It can similarly encourage businesses to hold back on the purchase of new machinery. If consumers and businesses spend less, the chronic problem of overproduction becomes worse. Profits fall, investment declines, and unemployment rises. People then have even less to spend or are increasingly reluctant to do so because of growing insecurity. Such vicious circles could lead to a cumulative decline of economic activity.

A deflationary spiral of this kind has been observed in Japan. Soaring prices after decades of growth created a bubble that burst in the early 1990s. Since then domestic demand has been falling, prices have dropped, and unemployment has risen. As people became increasingly fearful about the future, they saved more and consumed less, while falling prices gave consumers an incentive to delay purchases. Attempts by the government to stimulate demand by reducing interest rates or increased public expenditure have failed so far to do so.

Japan initially appeared to be a special case, because the Japanese have historically saved a high proportion of their income, while the relative absence of a welfare state increased their 'rainy day' reliance on savings. There is clearly a vicious circle here, since lower spending results in higher unemployment, which generates more insecurity, which leads to more saving, and so on.

However, Germany too has recently been travelling down a deflationary path, even though a particular form of state welfare is well developed there. It has been argued that Germany is also a special case, either because of the costs of its reunification or the rigidities of its labour market. If two large and rather different economies are caught in deflationary circles, that does, none the less, suggest that this may be a more general problem.

In which case, why have such circles not developed in Britain? Consumer spending has apparently 'defied gravity' by continuing to increase. Expenditure on services, where prices have continued to rise, has been particularly important in maintaining employment in the labour-intensive service sector. The expansion of credit has played a key part in this growing consumption. The highly developed and very competitive British financial services industry has found new ways of selling credit, most recently by lending on the security of the increased value of people's houses. The problem of overproduction has been temporarily solved by a debt-fuelled overconsumption.

Debts cannot, however, expand indefinitely. People's willingness to borrow and spend can be changed suddenly if their circumstances change, and in Britain their circumstances are indeed clearly changing, with higher taxation, higher university fees, and worsening pension prospects. Increasing debt can only sustain demand for a time and there is the risk of a very sudden and large contraction when people cut their spending because they can no longer afford to borrow and have high repayments to make.

The bursting of the ICT and related stock market bubbles made these problems that much worse. As the bubbles inflated, new products, high earnings in the financial services industry, and the euphoria of increasing personal capital stimulated spending. Then the bursting of the bubble resulted in the contraction of employment and earnings in the communications industry and financial services. It also resulted in many people losing a large chunk of their savings *and* expecting smaller pensions, because pension funds have made big losses. A similar sequence may follow if the bubble in house prices also bursts.

All this may be expected to shift people's priorities from spending to saving. Furthermore, governments with expenditure plans based on the increasing tax revenues generated by growth have now to reduce spending or increase tax rates or borrow more, all of which will have consequences that reduce consumer demand. Declining consumption would further widen the gap between production and consumption and result in the problem of overproduction/underconsumption becoming progressively worse.

A final crisis?

The capitalist world economy's failure to enter a new period of sustained and stable growth, the scandals at Enron and WorldCom, the bursting of various financial bubbles, together with predictions of a future slide into deflation, have led some to suggest that the capitalist system is in danger of collapse, of sliding into some final crisis.

The scandals around Enron and WorldCom seemed particularly serious, since they threatened the normative basis of capitalism. If executives with share options were fraudulently inflating profits, company profit figures could no longer be believed, while the complicity of respected accountancy firms meant that audit mechanisms designed to prevent such abuses were not functioning. The similar failure of a raft of Wall Street banks to provide objective investment advice to their clients, who were steered towards companies in which the banks had interests, has also come to light. All this means that the information and advice on which investors rely cannot be trusted. Confidence in the operations of the capital market at the heart of capitalism has been shaken.

Scandals have, however, been a recurring feature of capitalism. The true capitalist is motivated by the amoral accumulation of money and this frequently drives particular individuals to bend or break the rules. It is only when bubbles burst that the fraudulent practices easy to conceal at times of expansion suddenly become visible. Governments then punish wrongdoers and increase regulation, as has been recently happening in the United States. Even if this cannot prevent new scandals occurring in the future – regulation always leaves ambiguities and loop-holes that allow sharp practice – it can sufficiently restore confidence to enable the market to operate.

The history of capitalism is, in any case, littered with crises. Periods of stable economic growth are the exception not the norm. The quarter century of relatively stable economic growth after 1945 may have shaped a generation's expectations about capitalist normality but it was not historically typical of capitalism. Crises are one of its normal features, for there are so many dynamic and cumulative mechanisms operating within it that capitalism cannot be stable for long. The separation of production from consumption, the competition between producers, the conflict between capital and labour, financial mechanisms that inflate and then burst bubbles, the switching of money from one economic activity to another are all sources of instability that have characterized capitalism from its very beginnings and will no doubt continue to do so.

Particular crises also come to an end. Thus, if overproduction is the problem, unprofitability leading to bankruptcies and closures will eventually reduce capacity. The more efficient producers that are left will become more profitable, expand production, employ more, and generate demand. A high rate of product innovation is one of the features of capitalist economies, and the creation of new products or new technologies will again stimulate growth some time in the future. While crisis has undoubtedly been a recurrent feature of capitalist economies, so has the astonishing capacity for the resumption of growth when the crisis has passed.

The other face of crisis in one part of the world is, anyway, growth somewhere else. Thus China's entry to the capitalist world economy, with its huge reserves of cheap labour, has increased international competition and threatened profitability and employment elsewhere. China itself, however, with nearly a quarter of the world's population, is potentially a huge source of world growth in the future. Cheap labour countries may not initially generate much consumer demand, but when growth takes place in them, higher demand for labour may be expected to lead to rising wages and greater consumption in the future. China is already becoming a big importer as well as a great exporter.

If there were a viable alternative to capitalism, the current symptoms of crisis might be more serious. Arguably, the great crisis of the 1930s was more serious for this very reason. At that time, the Soviet Union was industrializing on the basis of a non-capitalist, state-socialist economic system, while strong socialist movements in capitalist industrial societies were still gathering strength and seeking to engineer a shift to such a system. With the collapse of the state-socialist economies at the end of the 1980s and the decline of socialist movements, this alternative has gone.

That is not to say that the opposition to capitalism has disappeared. Anti-capitalist movements still exist and have made their presence felt in various ways, notably by organizing large demonstrations to coincide with international economic meetings, as at the 'battle of Seattle' in 1999 and the 'battle of Genoa' in 2001. Their weakness is, however, that although they attract considerable support, they do not present a viable alternative to capitalism in the way that socialism once, for a time at least, did.

Nor is this to say that alternatives have disappeared from the capitalist world economy. As Chapter 4 showed, there are distinctive national variants, and these have not been forced by globalization into some common mould. The economic dominance of the United States has admittedly resulted in the imposition of a free market version of capitalism on economically weak countries, particularly those seeking to borrow from US-dominated international organizations. Well-established capitalist economies have, however, maintained their political and institutional distinctiveness and continue to provide alternative models. What matters here is not just what the established alternatives have on offer, interesting though this may be, but a recognition of the fact that distinct national variants have always existed and continue to operate within the capitalist world economy.

The search for an alternative *to* capitalism is fruitless in a world where capitalism has become utterly dominant, and no final crisis is in sight or, short of some ecological catastrophe, even really conceivable. The socialist alternative has lost its credibility, while contemporary anti-capitalist movements seem to lead nowhere, because of their failure to provide a credible and constructive alternative that is compatible with existing patterns of production and consumption. Those who wish to reform the world should focus on the potential for change *within* capitalism. There are different capitalisms, and capitalism has gone through many transformations. Reform does, however, require an engagement with capitalism and cannot be accomplished by movements that stand outside it and merely demonstrate against it.

References

Chapter 1

F. Braudel, *The Wheels of Commerce* (William Collins Sons and Co., 1982)

K. N. Chaudhuri, *The English East India Company 1600–1640* (Frank Cass and Co., 1965)

J. Gapper and N. Denton, *All That Glitters: The Fall of Barings* (Hamish Hamilton, 1996)

C. H. Lee, *A Cotton Enterprise 1795–1840: A History of M'Connel and Kennedy* (Manchester University Press, 1972)

H. de Soto, *The Mystery of Capital* (Bantam Press, 2000)

E. P. Thompson, 'Time, work-discipline, and industrial capitalism', *Past and Present*, vol. 38 (1967), pp. 56–97

Chapter 2

R. Brenner, 'Agrarian Class Structure and Economic Development in Pre-Industrial Europe', *Past and Present*, vol. 97 (1982)

C. M. Cipolla, *Before the Industrial Revolution: European Society and Economy 1000–1700*, 3rd edn. (Routledge, 1997)

H. Kamen, *The Iron Century: Social Change in Europe, 1550–1660* (Weidenfeld and Nicolson, 1971)

M. Morishima, *Why has Japan 'Succeeded'?* (Cambridge University Press, 1982)

H. Trevor-Roper, *Religion, the Reformation, and Social Change*, 2nd edn. (Macmillan, 1972)

M. Weber, *The Protestant Ethic and the Spirit of Capitalism* (George Allen and Unwin, 1930)

E. M. Wood, *The Origin of Capitalism* (Monthly Review Press, 1999)

Chapter 3

A. Gamble, *The Free Economy and the Strong State: The Politics of Thatcherism*, 2nd edn. (Macmillan, 1994)

A. Giddens, *The Third Way: The Renewal of Social Democracy* (Polity, 1998)

J. Percy-Smith and P. Hillyard, 'Miners in the arms of the law: a statistical analysis', *Journal of Law and Society*, 12 (1985)

D. Yergin and J. Stanislaw, *The Commanding Heights: The Battle for the World Economy* (Simon and Schuster, 1998)

Chapter 4

A. D. Chandler, *Scale and Scope: The Dynamics of Industrial Capitalism* (Harvard University Press, 1990)

D. Coates, *Models of Capitalism: Growth and Stagnation in the Modern Era* (Polity Press, 2000)

R. P. Dore, *Stock Market Capitalism: Welfare Capitalism: Japan and Germany versus the Anglo-Saxons* (Oxford University Press, 2000)

C. Johnson, *MITI and the Japanese Miracle: The Growth of Industrial Policy, 1925–1975* (Stanford University Press, 1982)

Organization for Economic Cooperation and Development, *Benefits and Wages* (OECD Indicators, 2002)

Organization for Economic Cooperation and Development, *Economic Survey of Sweden* (2002)

D. Swank, *Global Capital, Political Institutions, and Policy Changes in Developed Welfare States* (Cambridge University Press, 2002)

F. B. Tipton, 'Government policy and economic development in Germany and Japan: a sceptical evaluation', *The Journal of Economic History*, 41 (1981)

Chapter 5

M. Castells, 'Information technology and global capitalism', in *On the Edge: Living with Global Capitalism*, ed. W. Hutton and A. Giddens (Jonathan Cape, 2000)

D. Coates, *Models of Capitalism: Growth and Stagnation in the Modern Era* (Polity Press, 2000)

P. Dicken, *Global Shift: The Internationalization of Economic Activity*, 3rd edn. (Paul Chapman, 1998)

J. Gray, *False Dawn: The Delusions of Global Capitalism* (Granta, 1998)

V. Shiva, 'The world on the edge', in *On the Edge: Living with Global Capitalism*, ed. W. Hutton and A. Giddens (Jonathan Cape, 2000)

J. Stiglitz, *Globalization and its Discontents* (Allen Lane, 2002)

United Nations Development Programme, *Human Development Report* (Oxford University Press, 2001)

Chapter 6

G. Arrighi, *The Long Twentieth Century: Money, Power, and the Origins of Our Times* (Verso, 1994)

E. Hobsbawm, *Age of Extremes: The Short Twentieth Century* (Abacus, 1994)

K. Marx and F. Engels, *The Communist Manifesto* ([1848] Penguin, 1967)

Organization for Economic Cooperation and Development, *The New Economy: Beyond The Hype* (2001)

S. Schama, *The Embarrassment of Riches* (Collins, 1987)

Further reading

Chapter 1

Fernand Braudel's three-volume *Civilization and Capitalism: 15th–18th Centuries* (William Collins, 1982–4) is a wonderful source of insight into the nature and early history of capitalism. See especially Volume II, chapters 3 and 4, and the Conclusion to Volume III. On the methods used to discipline and control labour in 19th-century factories, see S. Pollard, *The Genesis of Modern Management* (Penguin, 1968). The excesses of the speculative capitalism of recent years are chronicled by Susan Strange in *Casino Capitalism* (Manchester University Press, 1997). To read further about Marx (and Max Weber) on capitalism, see Derek Sayer's *Capitalism and Modernity* (Routledge, 1991). Hernando de Soto's book, *The Mystery of Capital* (Bantam Press, 2000), contains intriguing reflections, going back to the writings of Adam Smith and Karl Marx, on the character of capitalism and its failure to emerge locally in Third-World countries.

Chapter 2

Ellen Meiksins Wood, *The Origin of Capitalism* (Monthly Review Press, 1999) provides a clear and forceful account of the origin of capitalism in Britain and is also the best way into the long-running Marxist debates on this question. In *The Transition from Feudalism to Capitalism* (Macmillan, 1985), R. J. Holton very usefully reviews both Marxist and non-Marxist theories. There is again much on the origins question in the Braudel volumes listed for Chapter 1. Although it is concerned with broader issues, Volume 1 of Michael Mann's *The Sources of Social Power* (Cambridge University Press, 1986) provides a theory of the origins of capitalism in feudalism and argues that Christianity and the political fragmentation of Europe were also crucial. Mann is much concerned with the distinctiveness of Europe, as is John Hall, who in *Powers and Liberties: The Causes and Consequences of the Rise of the West* (Blackwell, 1985) compares Europe with China, India, and Islamic societies.

Chapter 3

An influential version of the three-stage approach, though using different labels for the stages, was provided by Scott Lash and John Urry in *The End of Organized Capitalism* (Polity, 1987). The managerial revolution issue is discussed by John Scott, one of the leading researchers in this area, in *Corporate Business and Capitalist Classes* (Oxford University Press, 1997). In *Transformations of Capitalism: Economy, Society and the State in Modern Times* (Macmillan, 2000), Harry F. Dahms has very usefully collected together a number of classic texts on these issues. For a highly readable and globally extensive narrative of the latest transformation, see *The Commanding Heights* by Daniel Yergin and Joseph Stanislaw (Simon and Schuster, 1998).

Chapter 4

Will Hutton's *The State We're In* (Random House, 1994) and John Gray's *False Dawn: The Delusions of Global Capitalism* (Granta, 1998) both argue against the idea that globalization produces convergence, as does David Coates, in *Models of Capitalism: Growth and Stagnation in the Modern Era* (Polity, 2000), which lucidly examines all the major models and claims that each 'has stopped working'. Ronald Dore's *Stock Market Capitalism: Welfare Capitalism* examines the functioning and merits of the German and Japanese models, on the one hand, and those of Britain and America, on the other. While not covering anything like as much ground as the above, my *Labour Movements, Employers, and the State: Conflict and Cooperation in Britain and Sweden* (Clarendon Press, 1991) uses the notion of suppressed historical alternatives to explore the similarities and differences between Britain and Sweden.

Chapter 5

Vandana Shiva's 2000 Reith Lecture, *On Poverty and Globalization*, is available through the BBC's web page. For a comprehensive and clear general account of the recent development of global capitalism, see Robert Gilpin, *The Challenge of Global Capitalism: The World Economy in the 21st Century* (Princeton University Press, 2000). Susan Strange has chronicled the decisions (and non-decisions) leading to global monetary instability in *Casino Capitalism* (Manchester University Press, 1997). For a World Bank insider's perspective, see Joseph Stiglitz's book, *Globalization and its Discontents* (Allen Lane, 2002). For an outsider's call for fair trade rather than free trade, see George Monbiot's *The Age of Consent: A Manifesto for a New World Order* (Flamingo, 2003).

Chapter 6

On tulipomania, see Mike Dash's *Tulipomania* (Indigo, 1999) and Simon Schama's *The Embarrassment of Riches* (Collins, 1987). The best way into Marx's views on capitalism and crisis is to read Part One of *The Communist Manifesto* (originally published in 1848; among other editions, Penguin, 1967). Eric Hobsbawm provides a readable and perceptive account of the Great Depression, the postwar 'golden years', and the 'crisis decades' that followed in his *Age of Extremes* (Abacus, 1994). Gilpin (listed above for Chapter 5) sets recent crises in the context of global capitalism. The ups and downs of the dot.com story are chronicled in John Cassidy's *dot.con* (Allen Lane, 2002).

Index

Expand your collection of
VERY SHORT INTRODUCTIONS

Visit the
VERY SHORT
INTRODUCTIONS
Web site

www.oup.co.uk/vsi

➤ **Information** about all published titles

➤ News of **forthcoming books**

➤ **Extracts** from the books, including titles
not yet published

➤ **Reviews** and views

➤ **Links** to other **web sites** and main
OUP web page

➤ Information about **VSIs in translation**

➤ **Contact** the editors

➤ **Order** other **VSIs** on-line

POLITICS
A Very Short Introduction
Kenneth Minogue

In this provocative but balanced essay, Kenneth Minogue discusses the development of politics from the ancient world to the twentieth century. He prompts us to consider why political systems evolve, how politics offers both power and order in our society, whether democracy is always a good thing, and what future politics may have in the twenty-first century.

'This is a fascinating book which sketches, in a very short space, one view of the nature of politics … the reader is challenged, provoked and stimulated by Minogue's trenchant views.'

Ian Davies, *Talking Politics*

'a dazzling but unpretentious display of great scholarship and humane reflection'

Neil O'Sullivan, University of Hull

www.oup.co.uk/vsi/politics

HISTORY
A Very Short Introduction
John H. Arnold

History: A Very Short Introduction is a stimulating essay about how we understand the past. The book explores various questions provoked by our understanding of history, and examines how these questions have been answered in the past. Using examples of how historians work, the book shares the sense of excitement at discovering not only the past, but also ourselves.

www.oup.co.uk/vsi/history

MARX

A Very Short Introduction

Peter Singer

Peter Singer has succeeded in identifying the central vision that unifies Marx's thought. He thus makes it possible, in remarkably few pages, for us to grasp Marx's views as a whole, rather than as an economist or a social scientist. He explains alienation, historical materialism, the economic theory of Capital and Marx's ideas of communism in plain English, and concludes with an assessment of Marx's legacy.

'An admirably balanced portrait of the man and his achievement.'

Philip Toynbee, *Observer*

www.oup.co.uk/isbn/0-19-285405-4

THE EUROPEAN UNION
A Very Short Introduction
John Pinder

John Pinder writes with expert knowledge of the European
Union, explaining the interplay between governments and
federal elements in the institutions; consensus over the
single market and the environment; and conflicts over
agriculture, social policies, the Euro and frontier controls.
He shows how the Union relates to its European
neighbours, The United States, and the rest of the world,
and outlines the choices that lie ahead. He is clear about
his federalist orientation, presents the arguments fairly, and
is scrupulous about the facts. This is quite simply the best
short book on the subject.

'This short, detailed yet splendidly readable book . . . is a
must for anyone seeking to understand the European
Union, its origins, development, and possible future.'

Michael Palliser

'. . . indispensable not only for beginners but for all
interested in European issues. Pithy, lucid, accessible it
covers recent history, institutions, and policies, as well as
future developments.'

Rt. Hon. Giles Radice, MP

www.oup.co.uk/isbn/0-19-285375-9

PHILOSOPHY
A Very Short Introduction
Edward Craig

This lively and engaging book is the ideal introduction for anyone who has ever been puzzled by what philosophy is or what it is for.

Edward Craig argues that philosophy is not an activity from another planet: learning about it is just a matter of broadening and deepening what most of us do already. He shows that philosophy is no mere intellectual pastime: thinkers such as Plato, Buddhist writers, Descartes, Hobbes, Hume, Hegel, Darwin, Mill and de Beauvoir were responding to real needs and events – much of their work shapes our lives today, and many of their concerns are still ours.

'A vigorous and engaging introduction that speaks to the philosopher in everyone.'

John Cottingham, University of Reading

'addresses many of the central philosophical questions in an engaging and thought-provoking style ... Edward Craig is already famous as the editor of the best long work on philosophy (the Routledge Encyclopedia); now he deserves to become even better known as the author of one of the best short ones.'

Nigel Warburton, The Open University

www.oup.co.uk/isbn/0-19-285421-6